# THEO'S
# FAMILY
# KITCHEN

# THEO'S
# FAMILY
# KITCHEN

## 75 RECIPES FOR FAST,
## FEEL GOOD FOOD AT HOME

**THEO A. MICHAELS**

photography by Mowie Kay

RYLAND PETERS & SMALL
LONDON • NEW YORK

DEDICATION
To my wife Anna and kids Eva, Lex and Luca
– you are my world. x

*Senior Designer* Megan Smith
*Creative Director* Leslie Harrington
*Editorial Director* Julia Charles
*Production Manager* Gordana Simakovic

*Food Stylist* Libby Silbermann
*Prop Stylist* Hannah Wilkinson
*Indexer* Hilary Bird

MIX
Paper from
responsible sources
FSC® C106563

Published in 2023
by Ryland Peters & Small
20–21 Jockey's Fields
London WC1R 4BW
and
341 E 116th St
New York NY 10029
www.rylandpeters.com

Text copyright © Theo A. Michaels 2023
Design and photographs copyright
© Ryland Peters & Small 2023

ISBN: 978-1-78879-558-6

10 9 8 7 6 5 4 3 2 1

Printed and bound in China.

CIP data from the Library of Congress has
been applied for. A CIP record for this book
is available from the British Library.

NOTES
• Both British (metric) and American (imperial
plus US cups) measurements are included
in these recipes; however, it is important to
work with one set of measurements and not
alternate between the two within a recipe.
• Spoon measurements are level – a tablespoon
is 15 ml and a teaspoon 5 ml.
• Uncooked or partially cooked eggs should
not be served to the very old, frail, young
children, pregnant women or those with
compromised immune systems.
• Herbs used in the recipes are fresh unless
specified as dry.
• When a recipe calls for the grated zest of
citrus fruit, buy unwaxed fruit and wash well
before using. If you can only find treated fruit,
scrub well in warm soapy water before using.
• Always sterilize jars to be used for storing
homemade preserves and sauces before use.

# CONTENTS

# INTRODUCTION

Welcome to *Theo's Family Kitchen*. I've wanted to write this book for a while – not only to provide a manual on creating delicious homecooked family meals but also to create the sort of book I could pass on to my own kids and know they'll be armed with not only a collection of tasty and reliable recipes but also a blueprint for learning some basic cooking skills. That is why the first section on How to Cook the Perfect... was so important to me to include – the recipes and techniques you will find here are the building blocks of most of the dishes we make at home. From what you can do with eggs, how to make a white sauce, serve perfect potato and rice sides and roast an amazing chicken. And much more besides.... like how to cook a proper basic tomato sauce and what to then add to instantly take it from the Mediterranean to Mexico, or India or elsewhere – simple tweaks that create a labyrinth of taste opportunities, demonstrating that once you've mastered the basics you can do anything!

But there's more... our family life is hectic; three kids running about, a dog (that barks at air) chasing after them, my wife and I juggling the demands of work and home (all the while moonlighting as a kids' taxi service – unpaid might I add!). But amid the chaos of our everyday home life, meals are the eye of the storm; when we all come together to eat and enjoy each other's company and experience a moment of calm. Sorry, who am I kidding? Our dinnertimes are hardly calm, but we're together! Feeding my family unprocessed, homecooked meals when we do stop to eat is important to me and I want to pass on my knowledge so you can do the same.

Many of my previous cookbooks delve into the food associated with my Greek Cypriot heritage, celebrate village-style food from across the various Mediterranean countries, or are about creating grand sharing feasts, but this is a collection of our family recipes gathered in one place for you to prepare for your own family. These are the actual dishes we cook at home; inspired by cuisines from all over the world but with a common thread of being accessible, delicious and easy to recreate. We kick off with Weeknight Heroes – this is your go-to chapter for getting through the week with mouth-watering recipes that are quick and easy solutions for the time-starved. Relaxed Weekends follows and provides you with a delectable selection of recipes for when you've got more time to spend in the kitchen and may also be feeding a few extra mouths. Try my slow-cooked porchetta or my insanely good cool-box sous vide rack of lamb. Next, Family Fakeaways is full of sure-fire hits for when you want to recreate the fun of your favourite take-outs at home; from an Indian-inspired curry feast or Chinese-style noodle bowls to classic Friday-night fish and chips and gyro-style kebabs. The Salads & Sides chapter offers new and fresh ideas for tasty accompaniments to slip into any meal (or on occasion just enjoy on their own!). Finally, I couldn't resist including a selection of indulgent desserts for when you want to treat yourselves (and may I say, my lemon and thyme meringue pie is one of our all-time favourites – it never has a chance to cool down when it comes out of the oven as we eat it IMMEDIATELY!).

Food is one of the most important things that brings people together. When we share a meal, we're not just eating; we're also creating memories, building relationships and celebrating life. That's why I'm so passionate about this book and sharing our recipes with you. As with all my previous books, I want this to be a guide, not a set of rigid instructions and I hope that these recipes will become a part of your family's weekly routine. I hope that you'll gather around the table with your loved ones, make some noise, have a heated debate, and enjoy these meals together – creating your own memories and traditions as you cook from *Theo's Family Kitchen*.

# HOW TO COOK THE
# PERFECT...

It's always fun to follow new recipes, but every busy family cook will benefit from having a good repertoire of solid kitchen skills up their sleeve. If you can master the everyday stuff, by which I mean rustling up breakfast eggs, cooking veg well, making perfect potato and rice sides, knowing how to whip up a tasty sauce, roasting a chicken and making a decent shortcrust pastry, you are already ahead of the game!

## EGGS

Here's a quick guide on getting the most out of your morning (or brunch, or supper) eggs. The following methods were tested using UK medium/US large eggs, each weighing about 65 g/2¼ oz. Regardless of how you are cooking your eggs, the general rule is the fresher the better. Buy the best quality you can afford (but always free-range) or find friends with chickens – you'll never get nicer eggs than ones freshly laid next door! Always store eggs at room temperature rather than in the fridge.

*TOP TIPS FOR BOILED EGGS*
» A grey ring around the yolk of your boiled egg may be unsightly but it is perfectly harmless. To avoid it, don't overcook eggs; even if you want them hard boiled/hard cooked, 12 minutes is long enough!
» For ease of peeling, it's best to cool your boiled eggs as soon as they finish cooking; keep them submerged in cold water and peel them before they fully cool down.
» Store boiled eggs in your fridge; unpeeled they can last a few days, once peeled they should be eaten within 48 hours.

## BOILED EGGS

Boiling an egg is not an exact science! There are lots of variables, ranging from how large your eggs are to what the ambient temperature is that will affect the outcome. The following guidelines should, however, get you as close to perfection as possible.

Bring a saucepan of salted water to a rolling boil. Lower the eggs into the water, they should be at least 2 cm/1 in. under the surface of the water. Once they are submerged, maintain the heat until the water comes back up to a rolling boil (about 20–30 seconds), then reduce the heat to low so it's just keeping the water warm with no bubbles.

Now set your timer as follows, depending on what result you are hoping for:
» 4–5 minutes for soft boiled runny eggs, perfect for dipping toast 'soldiers' into
» 6–8 minutes for semi-hard, fudgy yolk, ideal for salads
» 10 minutes for just under hard boiled, a whisper of softness, ideal for making egg mayonnaise
» 12 minutes for hard boiled, best for slicing

Remove the eggs from the pan, run them under cold water and peel. They will continue to cook in their shells so peel hard boiled eggs quickly and serve runny eggs straight away.

## POACHED EGGS

Ah, seemingly so easy but actually so hard to master!
I've given you my rigorously tested methods here.

> *TOP TIPS FOR POACHED EGGS*
> » Using fresh eggs makes a difference
> as the whites are firmer.
> » Cracking the eggs into a fine sieve/
> strainer to remove watery white leaves
> you with better formed poached eggs.
> » Don't boil the poaching water; it will
> break the eggs up.
> » A little drop of vinegar in the water
> helps and the taste isn't noticeable.

### STOVETOP METHOD

Fill a saucepan with water to a depth of at least
10 cm/4 in. and add 1 teaspoon white vinegar. Bring
to a rolling boil, then turn the heat down to a very
gentle simmer with bubbles barely forming.

Crack an egg into a small fine sieve/strainer just
long enough for any watery white to pass through,
then carefully pour the egg into a cup or ramekin.
Whisk the bubbling water in the pan in a circular
motion to create a vortex and then gently tip the
egg into the centre of it. Don't touch! Leave the
egg to cook for 3 minutes and then scoop out with
a slotted spoon. (If you prefer your eggs not runny,
leave to cook for 30 seconds longer.) Dab the
spoon onto a paper towel with the egg still in it
to remove some of the excess water, and serve.

### MICROWAVE METHOD

Fill a cup halfway with hot water and crack an egg
into it (no need to sieve/strain for this one). Place
into a microwave, uncovered, set to 800 watts and
microwave for 40 seconds. Scoop out with a slotted
spoon and serve. If you want the yolk firmer, pop it
back into the microwave, 5 seconds at a time, until
you are happy with it.

### POACHING MULTIPLE EGGS?

To cook a batch of poached eggs you can either
cook them individually using the stovetop method
(see left) for 2½ minutes each, then dunk briefly
into iced water and store in an airtight container in
the fridge for up to two days. When ready to serve,
re-poach in hot water for 30 seconds to warm. (This
is how we do it in our professional catering kitchen.)

Alternatively you can use a large high-sided frying
pan/skillet, again following the stovetop method
(left) but once the eggs are prepped and the water
has just stopped boiling, keep the water still, pour
the eggs into the pan and cook for 3 minutes. They
rarely come out as neat as when cooked in a vortex,
but you can trim the whites to neaten them up.

## SCRAMBLED EGGS

Where would we be without scrambled eggs? They take seconds to cook and once you've added some toast and the odd extra ingredient you have an instant and nutritious meal, any time of day.

**2 eggs, lightly whisked**
**a knob/pat of butter**
**sea salt and freshly ground**
**black pepper, to season**

**SERVES 1**

Get your frying pan/skillet really hot, add the butter and as soon as it melts pour in your whisked eggs – they should bubble immediately. Using the side of a fork or spatula, quickly drag the mixture back and forth around the pan, continually moving the eggs while they cook. After 1 minute, when the eggs have just firmed up, remove the eggs from the pan and serve. The eggs will continue to cook when removed from the pan so you want to remove them as soon as they have solidified to avoid overcooking. Season well and serve.

*TOP TIPS FOR SCRAMBLED EGGS*
» Use a really hot frying pan/skillet and drag the eggs around the pan as opposed to stirring them which creates little lumps.
» Don't overcook your scrambled eggs – you'll get watery liquid appearing in the pan and that's the eggs expelling their moisture. What's left is rubbery and can be a bit unpleasant to eat.
» You can add a splash of milk or cream to the whisked eggs to increase their volume and make them, well, creamier. My dad's secret ingredient is mayonnaise. He stirs in a tablespoon of it just before removing the eggs from the pan – he says once you do that, you'll never eat them any other way!

## OMELETTE/OMELET

Omelettes/omelets are great any time of the day and hugely versatile. Fill them with whatever you want – from grated cheese, to vegetables, ham or smoked fish etc. I've given you a recipe for a plain two-egg omelette here so you can add your choice of filling.

**2 eggs, lightly beaten**
**a knob/pat of butter**
**a sprinkle of chopped chives (optional)**
**sea salt and freshly ground**
**black pepper, to season**

**SERVES 1**

Add the butter to the pan/skillet and once it has melted pour in the beaten eggs, tilting the pan so the eggs spread evenly across the base. Using a spatula or side of a fork, gently drag some of the eggs from the edge of the pan towards the middle, then tilt the pan so the raw eggs spill into the empty space. Continue until the surface has started to solidify but is not fully cooked. This only takes a couple of minutes. Drop your filling (if using) in a straight line down the middle of the eggs, then run the spatula or side of a fork around the edge of the pan to ensure the eggs are not sticking. Carefully fold over both sides of the eggs to create a large cigar-shaped omelette. Roll it out of the pan onto your serving plate seam-side down, season well, sprinkle with chives (if using) and serve.

*TOP TIPS FOR OMELETTES/OMELETS*
» It's best to use a frying pan/skillet with sloping sides rather than a straight-sided one.
» Sauté or steam any vegetable filling first, and set aside until you are ready to use it – the eggs will take a fraction of the time your filling does.
» I find an omelette is good served with something sharp – hot sauce or a tangy fresh tomato salsa.

# RICE

There are of course hundreds of varieties of rice, all with their very own distinct personalities. I'm going to focus here on the most common ones most people have lurking in their cupboards and that I tend to use most often (see opposite). For me the two most frequently used methods of cooking rice is the absorption method (where rice is cooked and absorbs all the liquid with no need to drain) or cooking in lots of water like pasta and draining the rice at the end. Many people say some types of rice benefit from being rinsed first to remove excess starch, but just between me and you, since this is MY family cookbook I'm going to be honest; I rarely rinse my rice when cooking at home.

## ABSORPTION METHOD

This easy method is ideal for any long grain white rice varieties, including basmati. It works to a ratio of 2:1, water to rice. This very handily means that whatever you use to measure out your rice can be used to measure your water; just use the same vessel to measure twice the amount! (See Top Tip on portion size, right). Make sure you are using a lidded saucepan or pot large enough to contain the rice once it cooks and expands.

**320 g/400 ml/1⅔ cups white long grain rice**
**1 tablespoon vegetable oil**
**800 ml/3⅓ cups water**
**a pinch of salt**

**SERVES 4**

Add the rice to a saucepan with the oil, stirring and cooking it gently for 1 minute. Add the water, bring to a boil, stir once, cover, reduce the heat to a gentle simmer and cook for 12 minutes. Do not be tempted to lift the lid or stir the rice during cooking.

Remove the lid, lightly fluff with a fork (never a spoon) and rest for a couple of minutes to release the steam before serving.

## BOILING IN WATER METHOD

Fill a large saucepan or pot with water, salt generously and bring to the boil. Add your rice (ensuring there is at least 3 times the volume of water to rice), reduce the heat to a simmer and cover with a lid. Cook until the rice is al dente (soft on the outside with a little chew left on the inside); cooking times vary between 12–20 minutes depending on the rice. Once cooked, remove the pan from the heat, drain the rice in a sieve/strainer, then drop the rice back into the empty pan and cover with the lid until you are ready to use.

> *TOP TIPS FOR RICE*
> » Allow about 80 g/scant ½ cup uncooked rice per person. Quite conveniently; 320 g of rice (sufficient to serve 4 people) is about 400 ml/1⅔ US cups which is the same volume as a large mug or coffee cup – that's what I use at home to measure everything.
> » You can vary the flavour and colour of your rice by adding a chicken or vegetable stock/bouillon cube to the water first, or spices such as ground turmeric (which gives it a lovely yellow colour), star anise, paprika etc.
> » You can start by sautéing onions and garlic in your pan first then add the dry rice, or as in my recipe for Cuban-style Brisket (see page 98), I use the cooking juices of the meat instead of water to impart maximum flavour.

The rice I have in my cupboards:

### WHITE LONG GRAIN WHITE RICE (INCLUDING BASMATI)

This, the most commonly used type of rice, is three or four times as long as it is wide and makes a good every day all-rounder and accompaniment to other dishes. It cooks in 10–12 minutes using the absorption method (see left).

### BROWN LONG GRAIN BROWN (INCLUDING BLACK RICE)

As these rices are wholegrain and have their outmost layer of bran intact they can take up anything from 25–40 minutes to cook (check the package instructions). I cook them in about four times their volume of water on a low simmer with the lid on (topping up the water during cooking if needed) and then drain in a sieve/strainer. They have a lovely chewy texture and are deeper in flavour than white long grain rice varieties – they look fantastic when mixed with other rice or in salads.

### WHITE SHORT GRAIN RICE (INCLUDING ARBORIO, PAELLA AND PUDDING RICE)

These rices have rounder, short grains and a high starch content which is released when they are cooked and stirred. This creates a 'creamy' finish, making it the preferred rice variety for risotto; it is also excellent to use in a

paella. I always have a bag of it in my kitchen storecupboard. It can be cooked using the absorption method (see left) but needs to be left to cook for 20 minutes. If you are making a risotto or just generally cooking it uncovered on the hob/stove-top, you'll need to add more water to the pan and it will take around 30 minutes.

### WILD RICE

Wild rice is actually not a rice at all, but an aquatic grass and is quite expensive, which is why it tends to be mixed in with long grain white rice. This gives it a gentler flavour too, but if you are using it on its own it can be cooked as brown long grain rice (see left).

# POTATOES

Potatoes; how amazing are they? They can be cooked in so many different ways; sometimes as the star of the show, other times the best supporting act around. I've concentrated on everyday side dish potatoes here, and shared my tried-and-tested, favourite recipes with you that my family go to again and again.

## PERFECT MASH

We all love a good mashed potato, so here's a basic recipe with a few tips and then some variations for you to enjoy. The garlic isn't classic, but I always include it (it's very subtle), but leave it out if you prefer. I've listed some variations (see right) and however you make your mash, it always needs to be seasoned generously with salt and pepper.

**1 kg/2¼ lb. floury potatoes (see Top Tips, right), peeled, cut into 5-cm/2-in. chunks**
**2 garlic cloves , peeled but left whole, stalk end trimmed off (optional)**
**45 ml/3 tablespoons whole/full-fat milk, warmed**
**50 g/3½ tablespoons butter, plus extra to serve**
**sea salt and ground white pepper, to season**

**SERVES 4**

Bring a large saucepan of salted water to the boil. Drop in the potatoes and garlic cloves and cook for 15–20 minutes, until a knife can be inserted without much resistance but the potatoes haven't started to crack. Drain the potatoes, discarding the cooking liquid, and return them to the hot, dry saucepan you just cooked them in and leave for a few minutes to let the steam escape and dry. Use a potato masher to break up the potatoes; they can be chunky at this stage. Add salt and pepper to taste (it's easier to season now than when fully mashed), pour in the warm milk and add the butter. Continue to mash until smooth, adding more milk if needed. Serve with a knob/pat of butter on top.

*TOP TIPS FOR PERFECT MASH*
» Use floury potatoes such as Yukon Gold, Maris Piper, King Edward – stay away from waxy varieties for a proper mash.
» Peel your potatoes; and cut into large even chunks; this helps them cook evenly but also reduces the surface area to absorb water.
» Don't overcook your potatoes; as soon as they are tender remove from the pan, if you overcook them they'll start to break down and soak up the water which does nothing except dilute their flavour and compromise their consistency.
» Leave your potatoes to steam dry before mashing (see recipe method, left).
» Try using a ricer or potato masher attachment on your food processor – just don't blend; it'll turn into wallpaper paste!

*VARIATIONS*
» Whole grain mustard stirred in at the end for a mustardy mash

» Chopped fresh herbs (parsley is good)

» Grated hard cheese stirred in and finished with lots of grated cheese on top (Gruyère or Parmesan are both delicious)

» Crushed garlic with lashings of extra virgin olive oil and a pinch of chopped fresh parsley to create a quick Greek-inspired skordalia

» Vary the flavouring by warming the milk through with different spices or herbs (such as mustard seeds or bay leaves)

» Irish Champ (see recipe page 16)

» Bubble & Squeak (see recipe page 16)

## BUBBLE & SQUEAK

I couldn't not include a good ol' fashioned Bubble & Squeak. It is a perfect way to use up leftover veg but it should ALWAYS include cabbage, so cook some fresh if you don't have any that's already good to go!

**1 quantity Perfect Mash (see page 15), prepared up to the point where you add the milk**
**½ the volume of mash of leftover cooked vegetables, diced to 1.5-cm/½-in. pieces**
**1 white onion, diced**
**1 egg, lightly beaten**
**25 g/1¾ tablespoons butter**
**2 tablespoons olive oil**
**60 g/½ cup plain/all-purpose flour**
**salt and freshly ground black pepper, to season**

**SERVES 4**

Add the mashed potato, vegetables and egg to a large mixing bowl and season with salt and pepper.

Sauté the onion in a frying pan/skillet with a splash of oil for 5 minutes, until caramelized. Tip into the same bowl as the mash and vegetables. Mix until everything is well combined.

Return the pan to the heat with the butter and olive oil. Take a tangerine-sized portion of the mixture, and using your hands, form a patty that is 2 cm/1 in. thick. Dust in the flour and place into the hot pan. Flatten with a spatula to ensure good contact is made with the pan – you want a nice crust – fry for about 5 minutes without moving before carefully turning over and frying the other side for 3 minutes. Don't worry if it cracks a little; this is meant to be a bit rough and ready. Repeat until all patties are cooked.

Serve hot with a fried egg on top if liked!

## IRISH CHAMP

This is a delicious mash variation with the addition of finely sliced spring onions/scallions.

**1 quantity Perfect Mash (see page 15), prepared up to the point where you add the milk**
**3 spring onions/scallions, sliced**
**60 ml/¼ cup milk**
**salt and freshly ground black pepper, to season**

**SERVES 4**

Warm the milk in a small saucepan and add the spring onions/scallions. Blanche them and then remove and set aside, reserving the milk. Follow the recipe for perfect mash, using the reserved milk to pour into the potatoes. Stir in the wilted spring onions, check and adjust the seasoning and serve.

# GREAT CHIPS/FRIES

Twice-cook your chips! Trust me, the results are well worth the extra steps (also see Top Tips, opposite).

**1 kg/2¼ lb. white potatoes, unpeeled and cut into batons about 1 cm/½ in. thick**
**500 ml/2 cups vegetable oil**
**salt, to season**

**SERVES 4**

Add the vegetable oil to a large heavy-based frying pan/skillet set over a medium heat. Once the oil is shimmering, add the potato batons and fry for 10 minutes, until cooked through and golden, moving them around to avoid sticking together. Remove from the pan with a slotted spoon onto a paper towel, then turn the heat up to high until the oil is shimmering (about 180°C/356°F). Reintroduce the chips to the pan (in batches if you have to) and cook for a couple more minutes until they are extra crisp and warmed through; transfer to a clean paper towel, season with salt and serve.

*TOP TIPS FOR GREAT CHIPS/FRIES*

» The best potatoes for chips are floury
varieties; anything you would use to bake
will make great chips, such as Yukon Gold,
Maris Piper and King Edward.

» You need to cook chips in an oil with a high
smoke point such as vegetable, sunflower, rapeseed/
canola oil. Do not use olive oil, especially extra
virgin olive oil as it has a low smoke point.

## ROASTED CRACKED NEW POTATOES WITH ROSEMARY

Once you've tried my roasted cracked new potatoes
you won't go back to the standard ever again!

**1 kg/2¼ lb. new potatoes**
**60 ml/¼ cup olive oil**
**1 garlic bulb, sliced in half widthways**
**a few sprigs of rosemary**
**1 tablespoon sea salt**
**freshly ground black pepper**

**SERVES 4**

Preheat the oven to 220°C fan/240°C/465°F/gas 8.

Boil the potatoes whole for about 12 minutes or
until a knife can be inserted with minimal pressure
(but not overcooked and mushy).

Drain and leave to steam dry for a few minutes,
then pour into a baking pan, use the base of the
saucepan to crack the potatoes (don't move them),
drizzle over the olive oil, season with sea salt and a
few turns of black pepper. Slice the garlic bulb in
half widthways, nestle the bottom half into the
potatoes. Break off the other cloves and dot over
the potatoes. Roast in the preheated oven for
40 minutes or until they are very crispy. Remove,
rub the rosemary sprigs together to release their
aroma, brush over the potatoes, then nestle into
the potatoes and wait a few minutes before serving.

### WANT TRADITIONAL ROAST POTATOES?

If you want traditional roasties, take 1 kg/2¼ lb.
of potatoes, peel, halve lengthways, blanche in
simmering water (about 8 minutes), drain in
a sieve/strainer, give them a good shake to
rough up the edges and leave to steam dry.

Preheat the oven and a deep-sided roasting pan
to 180°C fan/200°C/400°F/gas 6 with just enough
vegetable, rapeseed or canola oil (or duck fat)
to cover the base. Once hot, tip in the potatoes
and turn them until coated in oil. Roast for about
45 minutes, until golden and crisp, turning them
over halfway through cooking time. Season as
soon as they come out of the oven.

# GREEN VEGETABLES

I'm going to focus here on green vegetables here as generally speaking they are what is most assessible and used most often as sides; such as cabbage, greens, fine green (French) beans, runner beans, broccoli, asparagus, peas and Asian greens. My preferred way of cooking most green vegetables is to pan fry and then steam in a frying pan/skillet. This avoids overcooking, keeps in all their goodness and offers the opportunity to add different flavours while cooking (something you don't get when boiling your veg in water). (See photograph opposite.)

## GREEN VEGETABLE MEDLEY

Follow this method, swapping the selection of greens to suit what is in season, what you have to hand or what you fancy.

**1 garlic clove, sliced**
**2 tablespoons olive oil**
**1 small head of broccoli, broken into florets**
**½ sweetheart cabbage, shredded**
**180 g/6½ oz. green (French) beans or prepared runner beans**
**150 ml/⅔ cup chicken or vegetable stock (see page 29), white wine or water**
**125 g/1 cup frozen or fresh peas or petits pois**
**30 g/2 tablespoons butter**
**salt and freshly ground black pepper**

**SERVES 4**

Fry the garlic for a few seconds in the oil in a frying pan/skillet. Add the broccoli, cabbage and beans and stir fry for 5 minutes. Pour in the liquid and add the peas. Keeping it on a high heat, cover immediately and leave to steam for 3–4 minutes. Remove the lid, letting the steam escape and continue on the heat until just a little liquid is left. Remove from the heat, stir in the butter and season with salt and pepper before serving.

## STIR-FRIED ASIAN GREENS

This is a great way to cook greens such as pak choy/bok choy (Chinese cabbage) and choy sum, as well as more robust kale and broccolini, also known as Tenderstem broccoli. (See photograph on page 4.)

**200 g/7 oz. choy sum, pak choy/bok choy or robust green vegetable of your choice**
**1 tablespoon sesame oil**
**1 tablespoon olive oil**
**1 garlic clove, sliced**
**½ chicken or vegetable stock/bouillon cube**
**1 teaspoon light soy sauce**
**salt, to season**

**SERVES 4**

Trim the stalks off the choy sum and cut roughly in half just below where the leaves start.

In a hot pan, combine the olive and sesame oils and the garlic. Stir for 30 seconds, then add the stalks of the choy sum, stir fry for a minute then crumble in the stock cube and add the soy sauce and about 45 ml/3 tablespoons water. Ensure everything is snug and leave to boil rapidly for 1 minute, then fold in the leaves. Leave to cook for 1 further minute. Transfer to a serving bowl and season with salt.

*TOP TIPS FOR VEGETABLE SIDES*
» Use chicken stock or wine to steam vegetables to add extra flavour.
» Soft green herbs such as coriander/cilantro, dill and mint can lift the flavour of cooked veg – just chop and sprinkle over your dishes before serving.
» Nuts add flavour and texture to simple veg sides– try green beans sprinkled with toasted flaked/slivered almonds or broccoli with toasted hazelnuts.

# FISH

Fish makes wonderful food for the family but it's all too easy to overcook (or undercook) it. Fear not, with a few handy tips and some proper guidance on cooking times based on the type of fish you are preparing, you'll be cooking fish like a pro chef in no time!

*TOP TIPS FOR COOKING FISH*

» The 10-minute rule: this is a rough guideline that applies to all methods of cooking fish. Basically it involves cooking fish for 10 minutes for every 2.5 cm/1 in. of thickness, measured at the thickest part of the fish. So, for example a fillet of fish 13 mm/½ in. thick – 5 minutes cooking time; a fillet of fish 5 cm/2 in. thick – 20 minutes cooking time.

» Pat your fish dry before pan frying and lightly season with salt for crispier skin and to stop it sticking to the pan.

» Flouring; to guarantee a crispy exterior you can lightly dust fish skin in seasoned flour; this helps make it crisp and also protects the flesh a little, helping to steam the inside.

» Fish skin contracts as soon as it gets hot, creating a cavity of air between the flesh and the skin that steams rather than fries the fish. This is what causes uneven cooking and soggy skin. As soon as you lay the fish skin-side down into a hot pan press down on it for a few seconds (either with your fingers or spatula) ensuring it 'sticks' to the pan.

## COOKING METHODS

### PAN FRYING

*Best for flatter fillets (seabass, haddock, etc.) and oily fish like mackerel.*

Pat your fish dry and season with a little salt all over. Heat a heavy-based frying pan/skillet until hot, add a splash of olive oil to the pan and once the oil is foaming, lay the fish in the pan skin-side down, pressing down immediately for a few seconds to ensure the fish makes full contact. Don't move it; wait a couple of minutes for a crust to form and the fish will unstick; if you try to move it before then the skin will stick and rip. Cook your fish fillet skin-side down in a hot pan for 80% of the total cooking time and then turn once to finish cooking on the flesh side for the last 20% of cooking time. The skin protects the flesh from overcooking, goes incredibly crisp and the flesh remains succulent. So, for a total cooking time of 10 minutes, cook for 8 minutes skin side-down and then turn over for the last 2 minutes. Look at the side of the fish and you will see it turning opaque as it cooks; when it's almost to the top of the fillet carefully turn the fish over for the last minute to finish cooking.

### PAN FRYING WITH STEAMING

*Best for slightly fatter fillets, salmon, cod loin etc.*

Follow the method for pan frying (see above) to the point where the fish has been pressed down and is making full contact with the pan – don't move it again, you want that skin to stay stuck. Halfway through cooking add about 60 ml/¼ cup liquid to the pan (water, wine, stock, as preferred), cover with a lid and let the steam finish cooking the fish. Remove the lid and carefully remove the fish to serve. If you don't move the fish from when you first pressed it down, the skin will still be crispy.

### ROASTING

*Best for whole fish on the bone, i.e. seabass or trout, meatier fish such as monkfish, and large pieces of oily fish, such as a side of salmon.* Preheat the oven to 200°C fan/220°C/425°F/gas 7. Place in a roasting pan or on a deep-sided baking sheet and cook uncovered, calculating the time based on the 10-minute rule (see opposite) You won't necessarily get crispy skin but you will get evenly cooked fish.

### POACHING

*Best for white or smoked fish fillets, such as cod or haddock.* Fill a deep-sided frying pan/ skillet with water, stock or milk. Place over low heat and warm the liquid to a gentle simmer – don't boil it; your fish will turn into mush; a gentle simmer is all you need. Add the fish and cook for 5–8 minutes, depending on thickness. Use a fish slice to carefully remove from the liquid.

### MICROWAVING

*Best for small portions of white fish, such as cod, or salmon.* Microwaving fish gives excellent results; place on a microwavable plate or bowl. Cover with cling film/plastic wrap (it needs to be air tight). Cook for half the cooking time calculated by the 10-minute rule (see opposite).

## HOW CAN YOU TELL IF FISH IS COOKED?

Regardless of the method you are using, always check your fish to see if it's done before serving it. Do this either by using a food thermometer (fish should be cooked to an internal temperature of 63°C/145°F), or do as I do and simply pull some of the flesh apart at its thickest point and gently try to flake it with a fork. It's done when it flakes easily and is opaque. If poaching fish such as cod in liquid, push a skewer through the thickest part – there should be no resistance. Always serve fish as soon as it's been cooked and don't be tempted to reheat it as it will overcook.

# HOW TO ROAST A CHICKEN

Knowing how to roast a chicken is a must-have cooking skill. Once cooked, a chicken makes not only a decent meal but creates endless opportunities for any leftovers, from sandwiches and stir-fries, to curries and pie fillings. The carcass can also be saved to make an incredible stock (see page 29).

## ROAST CHICKEN WITH GRAVY

**2-kg/4½-lb. whole chicken**
**45 ml/3 tablespoons olive oil**
**400 ml/1⅔ cups white wine or water, plus**
  **a few extra glugs of wine for the gravy**
**2 onions, sliced**
**a few sprigs of thyme**
**1 tablespoon plain/all-purpose flour**
**1 chicken stock/bouillon cube (optional)**
**salt and freshly ground black pepper, to season**

*a deep-sided roasting pan, large*
  *enough to take a whole chicken*
*aluminium foil and baking parchment*

**SERVES 4–6**

Preheat the oven to 180°C fan/200°C/400°F/gas 6.

Scatter the onions over the base of a high-sided roasting pan. Drizzle the olive oil over the chicken and season it inside and out with salt and pepper. Push the thyme sprigs inside the chicken and place it on top of the onions. Pour the wine (or water) into the pan. Loosely cover the crown with parchment paper (just to stop the foil sticking to the chicken) and then tightly cover with foil. Cook for 1 hour 20 minutes, then turn the oven up to 200°C fan/220°C/425°F/gas 7, remove the foil and parchment, add more wine or water to the pan if it's drying out, drizzle little olive oil over the top, a pinch of salt and continue roasting uncovered for a further 20 minutes or until golden brown. Remove from the oven, place the chicken onto a serving platter, cover loosely with the used foil and let rest for 20–30 minutes. While the chicken is resting, spoon off any excess fat from the pan and stir in the flour, scraping it around. Whisk in about 250 ml/1 cup freshly boiled water to loosen everything. Pour into a saucepan (along with the onions from the roasting pan) and top with a few glugs of wine; bring to simmer, stirring as you do while it thickens and cooks off the alcohol, pour in any juices collected from the resting chicken. You can crumble in a chicken stock cube at this stage for a richer gravy, if you wish. Pass through a sieve/strainer into a clean gravy boat or jug/pitcher just before you are ready to serve.

*TOP TIPS FOR ROAST CHICKEN*
**»** *Remove the chicken from the fridge 30 minutes before you are ready to cook:* This ensures even cooking and helps keep the meat tender, plus it doesn't reduce the temperature of the oven you've just heated up when you put it in.
**»** *Steam – then brown:* Adding a little liquid to the roasting pan and cooking the chicken covered steams the chicken, keeping it moist. Once almost cooked, remove foil to give it some colour and crisp up the skin, resulting in succulent meat every time. That's the way I cook a roast chicken and the same way I would cook a huge turkey.
**»** *Portion size:* Allow about 400 g/14 oz. chicken per person and multiply to work out the total weight you need to buy (but of course adjust this up or down depending on appetites).
**»** *Seasonal variations*: For a summery touch, squeeze a lemon over the chicken and pop the spent lemon halves inside the cavity along with 6 smashed garlic cloves. For an autumn/fall dish, add a selection of root vegetables (carrots, parsnips, etc.) and potatoes around the chicken to cook at the same time (see photograph opposite).

# WHITE SAUCE

A white sauce (or bechamel) is essential as the base for so many dishes, from a fish pie to lasagne, but also really useful if you just want to rustle up a good cheesy sauce or something a bit fancier with fresh herbs. Here's a foolproof basic recipe and then a few ways you can play with it (see Variations, right).

## BASIC WHITE SAUCE (BECHAMEL)

**50 g/3½ tablespoons butter**
**50 g/heaping ⅓ cup plain/all-purpose flour**
**500 ml/2 cups cold milk**
**a little freshly grated nutmeg (optional)**
**salt and ground white pepper, to season**

**MAKES 500 ML/2 CUPS**

Melt the butter in a saucepan set over a medium heat, then stir in flour and cook for a couple of minutes until it darkens in colour. Remove the pan from the heat, once it stops bubbling pour in 125 ml/½ cup of the cold milk and whisk until smooth. Pour in the remaining milk, whisk to combine and return the pan to the heat. Keep whisking as the sauce starts to thicken, then let bubble for a couple of minutes before removing from the heat. Season to taste with salt, pepper and a little grated nutmeg (if using). Basic white sauce done! (See right for some variations.)

*TOP TIPS FOR WHITE SAUCE*
» Using cold milk helps to prevent a lumpy sauce!
» If your sauce is too thick, simply add an extra splash of milk at the end of cooking to loosen it.
» If you are using milk to poach fish, for a fish pie for example, reserve the poaching milk as the base for your sauce as it will be infused with flavour.
» See page 104 for more general tips on thickening your sauces.

*VARIATIONS*

### CHEDDAR CHEESE SAUCE

**150 g/¾ cup grated/shredded Cheddar, or other hard cheese**
**a pinch of mustard powder (optional)**

Follow the recipe for Basic White Sauce (see left), omiting the nutmeg. Remove the pan from the heat and quickly stir in the grated cheese with a pinch of mustard powder (if using) – the residual heat will melt the cheese into the sauce. Cheddar is traditional but you can use Red Leicester for a brighter colour or even a spicy chilli/chile-flavoured cheese!

### CLASSIC MORNAY SAUCE

Follow the recipe for Cheddar Cheese Sauce (above), omit the mustard and replace the Cheddar with 75 g/⅔ cup. grated Gruyère and 50 g/scant ⅔ cup grated Parmesan.

### PARSLEY SAUCE

Follow the recipe for Basic White Sauce omitting the nutmeg. Remove from the heat and add 2 tablespoons chopped parsley and a squeeze of lemon juice.

### CREAM & CHIVE SAUCE

Follow the recipe for Basic White Sauce, omitting the nutmeg, remove from the heat and whisk in 2 tablespoons double/heavy cream and 1 tablespoon snipped chives before serving.

# TOMATO SAUCE

Where would we be without the classic tomato sauce? Here is my go-to recipe.

## BASIC TOMATO SAUCE

**2 tablespoons olive oil**
**1 large white onion, finely diced**
**2 garlic cloves, crushed**
**1 bay leaf**
**500 g/18 oz. good-quality passata (or canned whole plum tomatoes, sieved/strained)**
**1 tablespoon tomato purée/paste**
**½ teaspoon sugar**
**salt and freshly ground black pepper, to season**

**MAKES 500 ML/2 CUPS**

Add the oil to the pan and sauté the onion for 5–6 minutes over a medium heat, until it has softened and very light golden. Stir in the garlic, add the bay leaf and let them infuse the oil with their flavour for a minute.

Add the passata or canned tomatoes, tomato purée/paste and 200 ml/¾ cup water. Season well with salt and pepper and add the sugar. Simmer over a low heat for 20–30 minutes, until the sauce is glossy and thick, stirring occasionally.

Store in the fridge in an airtight container for up to three days or freeze to use another another time.

*TOP TIPS FOR TOMATO SAUCE*
» To get maximum flavour from your tomato sauce you need to use passata (sieved/strained Italian tomatoes) or good-quality canned tomatoes.
» Give your sauce plenty of time to cook and you'll be rewarded with a rich, sweet sauce; cook it too quickly and it will be watery and taste slightly acidic.

*VARIATIONS*

These obviously don't reflect the delicate nuances and flavours of each cuisine, but if you want to jazz up some home-cooked fare and swap that Bolognese for chilli con carne or make that Mediterranean chicken dish an aromatically spiced Indian version you've got some broad strokes to have fun with.

### MEDITERRANEAN SUNSHINE
Fresh parsley and/or basil, dried oregano, sliced black or green olives, capers.

### MEXICAN FIESTA
Chilli/dried hot red pepper flakes, fresh chilli/chile, chipotle chilli/chile, smoked paprika, cumin seeds, fresh coriander/cilantro, black beans.

### NORTH INDIAN SPICE
Curry powder, ground cumin, garam masala, turmeric, grated fresh ginger, coriander/cilantro.

### CHINESE TWIST
Soy sauce, Chinese five spice.

### SOUTH EAST ASIAN VIBE
Fish sauce, brown sugar, birdseye chillies/chiles, Makrut lime leaves, fresh mint, coriander/cilantro.

# HOMEMADE STOCK

A good stock forms the base of so many dishes, from soups to risottos. Making a stock is actually a straightforward process and here are four basic recipes that should cover all your needs. You can ring the changes by adding different whole spices or aromatics to add subtle flavour variations, such as fresh ginger and garlic, coriander/cilantro stalks, a splash of soy sauce for a Chinese feel, lemongrass, chilli/chile and fresh mint for hint of South East Asia or dried chilli/chile and even smoked sausage for a more Hispanic feel.

*TOP TIPS FOR MAKING STOCK*
» Roasting bones first will create a darker stock (ideal for beef stock, see page 30), while using uncooked bones will give you a lighter, creamy stock (ideal for chicken stock, see right).
» Make use of what you have; vegetable peel and trimmings a carcass from a roast chicken (see page 23) — basically, whatever you've got– just throw it in!
» If you use starchy vegetables (potatoes) your stock will be cloudy, which if you don't have a problem with, neither do I.
» Always start a stock with cold water; this helps you skim off any impurities.
» Don't be tempted to rapid boil a stock; it distributes the fats through the stock.
» Never salt your stock – as it reduces the salty flavour will intensify, if you add salt too the result may verge on inedible.

## VEGETABLE STOCK

You can buy what you need, but I recommend rummaging in your fridge and cupboards to use up any leftovers first. You really can add what you want to this; although using starchy vegetables (potatoes) will make the stock cloudy (see Top Tips, left).

**2 carrots, peeled, cut into 5 cm/2-in. chunks**
**2 onions, skin on, quartered**
**2 celery sticks/ribs, cut into 5-cm/2-in. slices**
**1 leek, cut into 5-cm/2-in. slices**
**2 bay leaves**
**a sprig of thyme and a few sprigs of parsley**
**6 black peppercorns**

**MAKES 1.5 LITRES/6 CUPS (ONCE REDUCED)**

Add the ingredients to a large saucepan or pot, fill with 2 litres/quarts cold water and bring to the boil. Reduce the heat and leave to simmer for 2 hours, uncovered. Once done, remove from the heat, leave to cool for 1 hour, then pass through a fine sieve/strainer.

## CHICKEN STOCK

You can use a leftover chicken carcass from a roast, (see page 23), ask your butcher for some chicken bones or pick up 1 kg/ 2¼ lb. of wings.

**1 kg/2¼ lb. chicken bones, carcass or wings**
**  (see recipe introduction)**
**1 carrot, peeled, cut into 5-cm/2-in. chunks**
**1 onion, peeled and quartered**
**1 celery stick/rib, cut into 5-cm/2-in. slices**
**2 bay leaves**
**a sprig of thyme and a few sprigs of parsley**
**6 peppercorns**

**MAKES 1.5 LITRES/6 CUPS (ONCE REDUCED)**

Add all the ingredients to a large saucepan or pot. Add about 3 litres/quarts of cold water, bring to the boil, then reduce to a simmer and leave for 3 hours, uncovered. Use a slotted spoon to skim off any impurities from the surface of the water as it heats up and during cooking. Once done, remove from the heat, leave to cool for 1 hour then pass through a fine sieve/strainer.

## BEEF STOCK

If you have leftover beef rib bones you can use these (or store in your freezer until you have enough to use), alternatively ask your friendly local butcher for some beef bones.

**2 kg/4½ lb. beef bones**
**1 carrot, peeled and cut into 5-cm/2-in. chunks**
**1 red onion, peeled and quartered**
**5 garlic cloves, peeled**
**2 bay leaves**
**a sprig of thyme**
**12 peppercorns**
**a 5-cm/2-in. cinnamon stick**

**MAKES 1.5 LITRES/6 CUPS (ONCE REDUCED)**

Preheat the oven to 200°C fan/220°C/425°F/gas 7.

Put the beef bones on a baking sheet and roast in the preheated oven for 45 minutes, then remove from the oven and leave to cool.

Add all the other ingredients plus the cooled beef bones to a large saucepan or pot. Add about 5 litres/quarts of cold water, bring to a boil then reduce to a simmer and leave, uncovered, for 5–6 hours. Use a slotted spoon to skim off any impurities from the surface of the water as it heats up and during cooking. Once done, remove from the heat, leave to cool for 1 hour, then pass through a fine sieve/strainer.

## FISH STOCK

For a fish stock the cooking time is only 20 minutes (and it will not reduce much) so it's a good idea to sauté the vegetables first to bring out their flavour. In the Western world only the bones and heads of white fish are used and not those of oily fish as doing so creates an unpleasant oily residue. If you want a very clean fish stock, then stick with white fish. However, I'm personally happy to use salmon in my stocks – it creates a slightly oilier brew, but it's packed with goodness and I enjoy the richer flavour.

**1 kg/2¼ lb. assorted fish bones and heads**
  **(gills removed from the heads)**
**250 ml/1 cup white wine**
**15 ml/1 tablespoon olive oil**
**1 onion, skin on, cut into eighths**
**2 celery sticks/ribs, cut 2.5-cm/1-in. slices**
**1 leek, cut into 2.5-cm/1-in. slices**
**1 fennel bulb, finely sliced**
**2 slices of lemon**
**1 bay leaf**
**a few sprigs each of parsley and dill**
**6 black peppercorns**

**MAKES 1.5 LITRES/6 CUPS (DOES NOT REDUCE)**

Wash the fish bones to remove any blood and cut away the gills from the fish heads if using. Sauté the onion, celery, leek and fennel for 8 minutes in a little olive oil just to release their flavour (try not to brown). Add the wine and reduce by two-thirds. Add all the remaining ingredients and add about 1.5 litres/6 cups cold water, bring to a simmer and leave, uncovered, for 20 minutes. Don't stir to avoid breaking up small bones. Remove from the heat, cover and leave to steep for another 30 minutes. Drain through a fine sieve/strainer or muslin cloth. If you are unsure whether or not you've caught all the small bones, leave the stock to cool and then gently pour it into a clean container leaving the sediment behind.

# SHORTCRUST PASTRY TART CASE/PIE SHELL

Sure you can buy shortcrust pastry in blocks, or a ready-made tart case/pie shell, but making your own is so quick, easy and cost effective.

**150 g/1 cup plus 2 tablespoons
    plain/all-purpose flour
a pinch of salt
60 g/4 tablespoons butter, cubed
1 tablespoon icing/confectioners'
    sugar (optional for sweet pastry tart/pie shells)**

*25-cm/10-in. tart tin/pie pan, lightly buttered
    and dusted with plain/all-purpose flour
baking beans or dried beans*

**MAKES 1 25-CM/10-IN PASTRY CASE/TART SHELL**

Preheat the oven to 200°C fan/220°C/425°F/gas 7.

Combine all the ingredients in a large mixing bowl. Work the flour and butter with your fingertips (or in a food processor) until you have a scraggy mess then add 15 ml/1 tablespoon water. This will immediately bring the dough together — add a tiny bit more if it doesn't come together. Knead until smooth and then wrap in clingfilm/plastic wrap and chill in the fridge until ready to use.

On a floured work surface, roll out the pastry until it is 3 mm/⅛-in. thick. Carefully lift it and place inside the prepared tart tin/pie pan, letting the edges of the pastry overhang to allow for shrinkage. Patch up any holes in the pastry at this stage.

Crumple a sheet of baking parchment, flatten it out onto the pastry and pour dried beans or baking beans evenly onto the paper. Bake in the preheated oven for 12 minutes. Remove from the oven, carefully remove the paper and baking beans and return the pastry case to the oven for 5 minutes to finish cooking the base. Leave to cool.

### NEED A TART CASE IN A HURRY?

Sometimes a biscuit base/crumb crust is all you need for a dessert – use any biscuit you like; digestives/graham crackers and Oreos tend to be my go to! Work to a ratio of 1:2 (i.e. use double the weight of biscuits/cookies to butter). Smash or blend the biscuits to a crumb, tip into a bowl and add a pinch of salt. Melt the butter, pour into the crumbs and mix to combine. Tip into a tart tin/pie pan and use the bottom of a glass to press down on the base until it is all firm and even. Chill for 30 minutes before filling.

# WEEKNIGHT
# HEROES

Quick, easy and tasty family meals

# RED LENTIL TARKA DHAL WITH HONEY ROASTED CAULIFLOWER

This delicious bowl of goodness has just enough spice to tantalize your taste buds. The roasted cauliflower has a nice crunch to it so adds a bit of 'bite' to the smooth and creamy lentil dhal it is nestled on. I use red split lentils as they can be cooked from dried in ten minutes without any soaking time.

Preheat the oven to 220°C fan/240°C/465°F/gas 8.

Place the cauliflower florets and leaves in a large mixing bowl, pour in the 2 tablespoons of olive oil and sprinkle over the curry powder, mustard seeds, chilli/chile powder and salt. Toss to coat the florets in the oil and spices Place them and their leaves on a large baking sheet, drizzle with the honey and pop into the oven for about 20 minutes, or until they start to crisp and brown.

While the cauliflower is cooking, make the dhal. Give the lentils a quick rinse, then put them in a saucepan with double their volume of water. Bring to the boil, then reduce to a simmer and cook uncovered for 10 minutes, skimming off any impurities as they cook. Once cooked they should have some texture but no crunch – if they are still too watery, spoon some of the liquid off. Leave to rest while you make the tarka.

To make the tarka, heat the 1 tablespoon olive oil and butter in a separate frying pan/skiller over a medium heat and sauté the onion for a few minutes until it softens. Stir in the garlic and ginger, quickly followed by all the spices and the salt. The butter will start to foam, at which point stir in the tomatoes and green chilli/chile. Leave to cook for 1 minute, then remove from the heat.

Finally, stir a third of the tarka into the cooked lentils, then divide into serving bowls. Spoon the remaining tarka over the top of the bowls. Pile the roasted cauliflower in the centre, scatter over some peanuts and chopped coriander/cilantro.

Serve with Greek yogurt for spooning and lime wedges for squeezing.

## ROASTED CAULIFLOWER

1 large cauliflower, broken into small florets (tender leaves cut in half)
2 tablespoons olive oil
1 tablespoon curry powder
1 tablespoon mustard seeds
a pinch of chilli/chile powder or hot smoked paprika
a pinch of salt
2 tablespoons runny honey

## TARKA DHAL

200 g/1¼ cups red split lentils
15 ml/1 tablespoon olive oil
50 g/3½ tablespoons butter
1 onion, finely sliced
3 garlic cloves, chopped
5-cm/2-in. piece of fresh ginger, grated
1 teaspoon ground turmeric
½ tablespoon ground cumin
½ tablespoon cumin seeds
½ tablespoon garam masala
½ tablespoon fennel seeds
1 teaspoon salt
6 baby plum tomatoes, halved
1 green birdseye chilli/chile, chopped

## TO SERVE

2 tablespoons toasted peanuts, crushed
a handful of coriander/cilantro leaves, chopped
200 g/scant 1 cup natural/plain Greek-style yogurt
4 lime wedges

**SERVES 4**

# EASY EGG-FRIED RICE

This ridiculously easy recipe is one I hesitated to include in this book as it is so simple! However, it is also one of my go-to dishes when we need to feed the family quickly – and I mean in minutes! It's also brilliant for using up any leftovers such as cooked vegetables and cooked meat; in short, it's a dish I think everyone should have in their repertoire so here it is. Oh, but there is one rule – you do need to use cold, cooked rice, either leftovers or store-bought cooked pouches of it.

Heat a splash of oil in a frying pan/skillet over a high heat and sauté the onions for 1 minute (don't move them around in the pan – you want the onion charred but not cooked through). After a minute, add the garlic, ginger, chilli/chile and spring onions/scallions and cook for a further 30 seconds.

At this stage you can add any leftover vegetables, prawns/shrimp or meat – keep stir-frying until everything is cooked or warmed through.

Stir in the petits pois, Chinese five spice and the cooked rice. Continue stir-frying for another minute until the rice is piping hot. And I mean piping...

Push the contents of the pan to one side, drizzle a little more oil into the empty space you have created and pour in the beaten eggs. Stir the eggs until fully cooked – do not be tempted to mix the eggs into the rice until they are fully cooked (that's important; it will make everything mushy if you do!).

Once the eggs are cooked and everything is mixed together, add the sesame oil, soy sauce, honey, vinegar and a good pinch of salt and stir everything together. Spoon onto serving plates and add a sprinkle of chopped coriander/cilantro to serve.

3 tablespoons olive oil
2 red onions, thickly sliced
3 garlic cloves, peeled and sliced
5 cm/2-in. piece of fresh ginger, chopped
1 red chilli/chile, sliced
3 spring onions/scallions, cut into 2.5-cm/1-in. slices
400 g/14 oz. prawns/shrimp or any leftover vegetables or meat (optional)
125 g/1 cup frozen petits pois (no need to defrost)
½ teaspoon Chinese five spice
800 g/6⅔ cups cooked rice (or 3 x 250-g/9-oz. pouches of cooked rice)
3 eggs, beaten
1 tablespoon sesame oil
2 tablespoons dark soy sauce
2 tablespoons runny honey
1 tablespoon cider vinegar
½ teaspoon salt
a handful of coriander/cilantro leaves, chopped

**SERVES 4**

# CRISPY CAULIFLOWER STEAK BURGERS

I love a veggie burger as much as the next carnivore, but actually these never fail to hit the spot! Cauliflower steaks are crispy fried, then oven roasted and lovingly served in a fluffy brioche bun with all the trimmings.

Preheat the oven to 200°C fan/220°C/425°F/gas 7.

Start with the cauliflower. Peel the leaves off (you can save those to roast another day), trim the stalk end, then cut four 4-cm/1½-in. thick slices straight through the stalk (this helps hold them together). Use both cauliflowers to get four steaks as the ends tend to fall apart – I freeze any offcuts or use them another day.

In a separate bowl, beat the egg with the milk.

Mix both flours together in a shallow bowl with all the spices.

When you are ready to start cooking, heat the vegetable oil in a frying pan/skillet set over a high heat (it's ready when a piece of cauliflower dropped in immediately sizzles but doesn't burn).

Dip the cauliflower steaks into the egg and milk mixture and then into the flour, ensuring they are fully coated. Fry the steaks (usually two at a time) in the hot oil for about 4 minutes on each side, or until golden and crisp (the crispier the better). Transfer to a wire rack sat on a baking sheet. Once all four steaks are fried, bake the cauliflower steaks in the preheated oven for 20 minutes. About 3 minutes before the end of cooking; lay a slice of cheese on top of each one and pop back in the oven to melt.

While the cauliflower is roasting, prepare the burger sauce by simply mixing all the sauce ingredients together in a bowl. Taste, adding more salt or gherkin vinegar until you are happy with how it tastes.

Once the cauliflower steaks are done, lightly toast the cut-side of the brioche buns under the grill/broiler (most of the time I don't bother). Slather the burger sauce on the bottom bun, top with a crispy cauliflower steak and then add lettuce, onion and tomato and finish with a little drizzle of bbq sauce or tomato ketchup.

2 small heads of cauliflower
1 egg
250 ml/1 cup whole/full-fat milk
130 g/1 cup self-raising/rising flour
50 g/½ cup cornflour/cornstarch
1 tablespoon smoked paprika
1 tablespoon ground cumin
½ teaspoon cayenne pepper
250 ml/1 cup vegetable oil
4 burger cheese slices

BURGER SAUCE
60 ml/¼ cup mayonnaise
2 tablespoons American mustard
1 gherkin, diced
1 tablespoon gherkin vinegar from the jar
½ teaspoon sugar
a pinch of smoked paprika
a pinch of salt

TO SERVE
4 brioche burger buns, split
1 Little Gem/Bibb lettuce, leaves separated
1 small red onion, thinly sliced
2 vine tomatoes, sliced
bbq sauce or tomato ketchup

**SERVES 4**

# PHILLY CHEESESTEAK CHIMICHANGAS

I spent a bit of time in New Jersey growing up so we were only ever a short trip away from South Street, Philly and the original cheesesteak so this recipe is inspired by those memories.

Heat a splash of olive oil in a frying pan/skillet set over a medium heat and sauté the onion and peppers for about 15–20 minutes until they are nicely caramelized. Remove from the heat, season with salt, pepper and the oregano and set to one side.

Meanwhile, prepare the meat. Cut each piece of steak in half, lay a piece in between two sheets of clingfilm/plastic wrap (or baking parchment) and use a meat hammer (or rolling pin as I do) to whack the steaks until they are as thin as you can get them (ideally about 3 mm/⅛ in. or less). Once flattened, season the steaks liberally with salt and pepper and roughly slice into 5-cm/2-in. wide strips.

Heat a frying pan/skillet to smoking hot, add a splash of olive oil and dump a handful of the steak strips into the pan, stir-frying as you do. Stir-fry only for a couple of minutes until most of the steak is cooked but there are still some pink bits. Use a slotted spoon to remove the steak from the pan. Continue until all the steak is cooked. I usually tip all the cooked onions and peppers back into the pan at the end to mop up any leftover flavours.

In a clean frying pan/skillet , fill with enough vegetable oil to cover the base by 2.5 cm/1 in. and set over a medium heat.

While the oil is getting hot, lay out a tortilla on the work surface and place some shredded white cabbage in the centre. Top with some fried steak, onions and peppers and finally a couple of slices of cheese. Fold the bottom part of the tortilla over the top of the filling, then fold both sides in and finally tightly roll it over so it seals (a bit like an envelope). Keep hold of it and dip in the egg wash, then carefully place into the hot oil, seam-side down. You must lay the egg-washed burrito seam-side down and leave it in place for 1 minute to stop it opening. Use tongs to turn it over after 1 minute and cook the other side for another minute until golden and crisp. Continue making and cooking the chimichangas until everyone has one.

Two chimichangas per person is usually ample but they also go well with a portion of chips/fries, if liked.

**a few splashes of olive oil**
**1 large white onion, thinly sliced**
**1 green (bell) pepper, thinly sliced**
**1 red (bell) pepper, thinly sliced**
**1 teaspoon dried oregano**
**500 g/18 oz. sirloin steak**
**about 500 ml/2 cups vegetable oil**
**¼ of a white cabbage, finely shredded**
**8 large flour tortillas**
**16 slices of Gouda cheese (or Provolone)**
**2 eggs, whisked**
**salt and freshly ground black pepper, to season**

**SERVES 4**

# SPICY SALMON & BEAN SKILLET

The flavour combination of salmon, spicy chorizo and sweet maple syrup serves brilliantly to create a dish that works both as a quick mid-week family meal or as something a bit 'fancy' for feeding friends. The trick here is using canned ratatouille and canned beans which speeds things up no end! Serve with fluffy rice (I prefer basmati with this, see page 12) to soak up the sauce.

Preheat the oven to 200°C fan/220°C/425°F/gas 7.

Heat the olive oil in an ovenproof frying pan/skillet over a medium heat and fry the chorizo slices for a few minutes to release their oils. Stir in the garlic and cook for another minute before adding the sherry and cooking out the alcohol for another minute.

Stir in 1 tablespoon of the maple syrup, the ratatouille, drained beans, chilli/hot red pepper flakes, salt, smoked paprika, tomato purée/paste, mix together and heat until it bubbles. Remove from the heat and stir in the sliced tomato.

Place the salmon fillet skin-side up on top of the beans, season with salt and pepper and drizzle over the remaining maple syrup (if it collects in pools around the salmon, gently mix this into the beans) and place in the preheated oven for 20 minutes.

Once the salmon is done, leave to rest in the pan for a few minutes, then garnish with chopped parsley and serve.

NOTE *If using individual salmon fillets, reduce the cooking time to about 15 minutes.*

2 tablespoons olive oil
2 chorizo cooking sausages, sliced
2 garlic cloves , sliced
60 ml/¼ cup dry sherry
45 ml/3 tablespoons maple syrup
2 x 400-g/14-oz. cans ratatouille
2 x 400-g/14-oz. cans borlotti/cranberry or cannellini beans, drained and rinsed
a pinch of dried chilli/hot red pepper flakes
1 teaspoon sea salt
1 teaspoon smoked paprika
1 tablespoon tomato purée/paste
1 vine tomato, sliced
500 g/18 oz. salmon fillet (about ½ a side of salmon)
a few sprigs of flat-leaf parsley, chopped

**SERVES 4**

# POTATO, CHORIZO & GOATS' CHEESE GALETTE

This is basically a posh pizza, only the bread base is replaced with puff pastry and sliced potatoes. I love the flavour contrast of spicy chorizo and jalapeño peppers with creamy goats' cheese.

Preheat the oven to 180°C fan/200°C/400°F/gas 6.

Mix together the melted butter, crushed garlic clove and thyme leaves and set aside.

Peel the potatoes, then slice widthways about 3 mm/⅛ in. thick (you could use a mandolin or a sharp knife – top tip: if cutting with a knife, shave off a slice from the bottom of the potato so it sits flat on your chopping board). Blanch the potato slices in a saucepan of boiling salted water for 3 minutes, then drain and carefully tip back into the empty saucepan (you want to avoid them breaking up). Drizzle over the butter-garlic mixture and season with salt and pepper and reserve.

Lightly dust the work surface and unroll the pastry sheet. Line a baking sheet with baking parchment and dust with with flour. Lay the pastry on top.

Lay the dressed potato slices neatly over the pastry (leaving a border around the edge) and slightly overlapping but no more than two layers high. Once done, squeeze out the chorizo sausage meat from their skins into bite-sized pieces all over the potatoes (they will shrink once cooked so be liberal). Scatter over the red onion and jalapeño slices and finally dot pockets of the goats' cheese over the top, finishing with pumpkin seeds/pepitas for a little crunch. Lift the edges of the pastry up and over the filling to make a raised side all the way around. Brush the edges of the pastry with beaten egg and bake for 35 minutes, or until the chorizo is cooked and the pastry is golden.

While the galette is cooking, dress the rocket/arugula with a little olive oil and cider vinegar. Once the galette is removed from the oven, place on a large rectangular chopping board to serve. Grab a handful of the rocket, shake off any excess dressing and place it on top of the galette. Top with cheese shavings, if using, and serve.

NOTE *any leftover goats' cheese can be folded through the rocket/arugula, as can a few shavings of cheese, if liked.*

25 g/1½ tablespoons butter, melted
1 small garlic clove, crushed
1 teaspoon thyme leaves or ½ teaspoon dried thyme
500 g/18 oz. potatoes
320-g/12-oz. ready-rolled sheet of puff pastry dough
plain/all-purpose flour, for dusting
6 chorizo cooking sausages
1 small red onion, thinly sliced
1 fresh jalapeño pepper, seeds removed and thinly sliced
150 g/6 oz. goats' cheese
1 tablespoon pumpkin seeds/pepitas
1 egg, beaten
a handful of rocket/arugula
2 tablespoons olive oil
2 tablespoons cider vinegar
a few Manchego or Parmesan shavings, to serve (optional)
salt and freshly ground black pepper, to season

**SERVES 4**

# SCANDI-STYLE MEATBALLS

In Scandinavian countries meatballs are served with buttery mash and a sour-sweet lingonberry sauce. Here is my speedy interpretation of this, with a rich creamy sauce and a dollop of cranberry sauce from a jar on the side to add the fruity notes.

Tear the bread into small pieces, put in a small bowl and pour over the milk. Leave it to soak.

In a large mixing bowl, combine the grated onion, dill (reserving some to garnish), minced meats, nutmeg, honey and egg. Season generously with salt and pepper and mix together. Gently squeeze out the excess moisture from the milk-soaked bread and add it to the meat mixture. Mix together and then roll into ping pong-sized balls.

Heat the olive oil in a frying pan/skillet and fry the meatballs for 3 minutes on each side until nicely browned. Transfer to a plate (they don't have to be fully cooked).

In the same pan, make the sauce. Add the butter and scrape the burned bits from the base of the pan. Stir in the flour and cook for 1 minute. Remove the pan from the heat and whisk in the beef stock, return the pan to the heat and whisk continuously for 2–3 minutes, or until the sauce thickens and bubbles. Add all the remaining sauce ingredients and reintroduce the meatballs to the pan (along with any juices). Gently simmer for 5 minutes, uncovered, to finish cooking the meatballs through.

Meanwhile, set a clean frying pan/skillet over a high heat and drop in a knob/pat of butter. Sauté the green beans for 2–3 minutes before adding a few tablespoons of water, cover the pan immediately and leave to steam for 4 minutes. Remove the lid and finish with little more butter and season with salt and pepper.

Arrange each portion of meatballs in a bowl of mash with some sautéed beans on one side. Spoon over the warm sauce, season with freshly ground black pepper and a sprinkle of dill, add a dollop of lingonberry or cranberry preserve and serve.

## MEATBALLS
1 slice of white bread
120 ml/½ cup milk
1 white onion, grated
6 sprigs of dill, chopped
250 g/heaping 1 cup minced/
    ground pork
250 g/heaping 1 cup minced/
    ground beef
freshly grated nutmeg, to taste
1 teaspoon runny honey
1 egg
2 tablespoons olive oil
5 knobs/pats of butter, for
    frying
salt and freshly ground black
    pepper, to season

## SAUCE
10 g/2 teaspoons butter
1 tablespoon plain/all-purpose
    flour
300 ml/1¼ cups beef stock
    (see page 30), or make up
    using a stock/bouillon cube
200 ml/¾ cup single/light
    cream
1 teaspoon Worcestershire
    sauce
1 teaspoon cider vinegar

## TO SERVE
250 g/9 oz. fine green beans,
    trimmed
Perfect Mash (see page 15)
Lingonberry preserve if you
    can find it, or cranberry
    sauce

**SERVES 4**

# OVEN-BAKED BROCCOLI & BLUE CHEESE GNOCCHI

I love superfast mid-week meals like this one. Gnocchi makes a nice change from pasta and I have found a way to turn them into a delicious ovenbake here. My cheat's recipe uses a can of broccoli and Stilton soup to make the sauce, making it really quick to prepare. Serve with a tomato and red onion salad.

Preheat the oven to 200°C fan/220°C/425°F/gas 7.

Heat the olive oil in an ovenproof frying pan/skillet over a medium heat and fry the onion, garlic and broccoli for a few minutes. Add 250 ml/1 cup water, cover and leave to simmer for 6 minutes until the broccoli is cooked and tender.

Remove the lid and add the gnocchi. Pour in the soup, season generously and stir to mix everything together. Bring to a simmer and once simmering, remove from the heat, stir in the cream cheese and place the pan in the oven for 12–15 minutes, or until the gnocchi is soft and cooked.

Serve with a tomato and red onion salad on the side (if liked) and some crusty bread for mopping up the cheesy sauce.

NOTE *If you've got any small bits of leftover blue cheese like Stilton lurking in the fridge you can crumble that in instead of adding the cream cheese, it will just give it a stronger flavour.*

1 tablespoon olive oil
1 onion, diced
1 garlic clove, chopped
1 small head broccoli, chopped
800 g/1¾ lb. ready-made
   gnocchi
400-g/14-oz. can broccoli
   and Stilton soup
50 g/1¾ oz. cream cheese
salt and freshly ground black
   pepper, to season

**SERVES 4**

# SAUSAGE MEAT & FENNEL SEED PASTA

A classic weeknight hero with a twist – the fennel seeds elevate this easy pasta dish, complementing the sausage meat with a subtle flavour that I personally find rather addictive!

Bring a large saucepan of water to the boil, crumble in the chicken stock/bouillon cube and add the pasta. Cook for 8 minutes or a few minutes short of the packet instructions. Once cooked, drain the pasta, reserving about 200 ml/generous ¾ cup of the cooking water.

Meanwhile, toast the fennel seeds in a dry frying pan/skillet over a medium heat, shaking the pan as you do. After a minute, pour the seeds into a bowl and lightly crush with a back of a spoon (or the end of a rolling pin or in a mortar with a pestle – they only need be broken, not powdered).

In the same pan, add a splash of oil and squeeze out the sausage meat from their skins into little bite-sized pieces; fry over a high heat for 4 minutes until a deep golden caramel colour. Pour in the white wine and scrape the pan and cook until the wine is reduced to just a drizzle. Add another little splash of olive oil, followed by the garlic, tomatoes, fennel seeds, chilli/hot red pepper flakes and season generously with salt and pepper. Cook for a few more minutes (you can at this stage press down on the tomatoes with the back of a fork to help them break down). Pour in the reserved cooking liquid and simmer over a high heat until reduced by half, giving the pan a shake every now and then.

Fold the pasta into the pan and cook for another minute, then remove from the heat.

Serve in pasta bowls with a drizzle of olive oil, a few turns of freshly grated black pepper, some grated Parmesan and a scattering of chopped parsley. If you have any toasted fennel seeds left over, you can sprinkle them on top too.

1 chicken stock/bouillon cube
320 g/12 oz. dried ribbon pasta, such as pappardelle or tagliatelle
1 tablespoon fennel seeds
light olive oil, for frying
6 pork sausages (about 500 g/18 oz.)
150 ml/⅔ cup white wine or water
2 garlic cloves, sliced
2 vine tomatoes, diced
a pinch of dried chilli/hot red pepper flakes
leaves from a handful of flat-leaf parsley, chopped
salt and freshly ground black pepper, to season
finely grated Parmesan, to serve

**SERVES 4**

# SINGAPORE-STYLE NOODLES

This is one of those recipes everybody needs in their repertoire. It may not be 100% authentic but a good noodle dish is a great way to hoover up a range of flabby vegetables from the bottom of your salad drawer, plus any meat or fish that needs using up or if you have cooked leftovers. You can also go vegetarian or vegan by swapping the eggs, prawns/shrimp and chicken for marinated tofu pieces, baby sweetcorn/corn and mushrooms.

Place the chicken breasts in a saucepan of cold water with a pinch of salt, bring to the boil, skim off any impurities, then lower the heat and poach the chicken for 5 minutes. Cover the pan with a lid, take the pan off the heat and leave for 10 minutes (this will cook the chicken while keeping it tender). Once cooked, remove the chicken from the water and shred or chop ready to be used.

Place the noodles in a large mixing bowl, submerge in boiling water, cover with a plate and leave for 8 minutes. Drain, rinse under cold water and leave the noodles in a colander or sieve/strainer placed over a bowl to drip dry. Run a knife through the noodles to break them down just a little and dust with a pinch of the curry powder.

Heat a splash of vegetable oil in a large frying pan/skillet or wok over a high heat. Once it starts smoking, add the onion and (bell) peppers and stir-fry for a minute. Add the garlic, ginger, beansprouts and prawns/shrimp and stir-fry for another couple of minutes (until the prawns are cooked and pink) before dropping in the shredded poached chicken and giving it a stir.

Add the drained noodles, stir-frying all the time to incorporate everything, and sprinkle in the turmeric, remaining curry powder, soy sauce and sugar. Push everything to one side of the pan, add a little more oil to the empty half and pour in the eggs, whisking fast as you do – they will cook in less than a minute; once cooked add the spring onions/scallions and sesame oil and mix everything together. Garnish with coriander/cilantro and serve.

2 skinless and boneless chicken breasts (about 300 g/10½ oz.)
250 g/9 oz. vermicelli noodles
1½ tablespoons curry powder mild
1 tablespoon vegetable oil
1 onion, cut into 1-cm/½-in. thick slices
1 red (bell) pepper, sliced
4 garlic cloves, sliced
a 2.5-cm/1-in. piece of fresh ginger, chopped
150 g/5½ oz. beansprouts
150 g/5½ oz. raw prawns/ shrimp
½ teaspoon ground turmeric
2 tablespoons soy sauce
1 teaspoon sugar
3 eggs, lightly whisked
1 tablespoon sesame oil
2 spring onions/scallions, sliced
a handful of coriander/cilantro leaves, chopped

**SERVES 4**

# PHO-MEN SOUP

Whilst travelling in Vietnam and Japan I did my fair share of slurping bowls of ramen and pho. Here I've brought the two dishes together – it isn't traditional or authentic, but instead I offer you my whimsical tribute to memory of those exciting flavours (and good times).

Place the steak in the freezer for 15 minutes, then remove and slice widthways (against the grain) as thinly as possible. Bring to room temperature.

For the soup, heat a drizzle of olive oil in a large saucepan over a medium heat and fry the onion and fresh ginger until charred (almost black). Add the garlic, cloves, coriander seeds, star anise and cinnamon stick and fry for a couple of minutes. Pour in the chicken stock, soy sauce, sugar and fish sauce and leave to simmer until you are ready to serve (you can do this for as little as 20 minutes or for a few hours for the flavours to really infuse).

While the soup is simmering, place the rice noodles in a large bowl and cover them in boiled water. Cover and let sit for 8 minutes, or until the noodles are hydrated. Drain, drizzle a little sesame oil over the top and set aside.

Gather the halved cabbage leaves together and, holding the stalk end, slide them into the saucepan of soup. Cook for 3 minutes, then use a slotted spoon to remove them, shaking off any spices.

When you are ready to serve, pass the soup through a sieve/strainer and return to the heat. Pile a portion of noodles into your serving bowls, add the cabbage leaves around the edge, the slices of raw steak and beansprouts in groups and ladle in the hot soup. Wedge in the coriander/cilantro, mint, sliced chilli/chile and place the egg halves into each bowl with a pinch of sesame seeds on each and garnish with a wedge of lime. You need to ensure the steak is covered by the hot soup which will cook it.

400-g/14-oz. sirloin steak
300 g/10½ oz. dried rice
    noodles
1 tablespoon sesame oil
12 Chinese cabbage leaves,
    halved lengthways
200 g/7 oz. beansprouts
a few sprigs each of coriander/
    cilantro and mint
1 red birdseye chilli/chile,
    finely sliced
4 eggs, boiled for 6 minutes
    (see page 8), peeled and
    halved
sesame seeds and lime wedges,
    to garnish

SOUP
olive oil, for frying
1 onion, sliced
a 5-cm/2-in. piece of fresh
    ginger, cut into matchsticks
2 garlic cloves , sliced
6 cloves
1 teaspoon coriander seeds
5 star anise
5-cm/2-in. long cinnamon stick
1.5 litres/6 cups chicken stock
    (see page 29), or make up
    using chicken stock/bouillon
    cubes
1 tablespoon light soy sauce
1 teaspoon brown sugar
1 tablespoon fish sauce

SERVES 4

# CHILLI CRAB LINGUINE
# WITH CRISPY BREADCRUMBS

A classic recipe of delicate crab meat with pockets of heat from the chilli/hot red pepper flakes and topped with a crunchy pangritata for a crunchy texture. You can substitute fresh crab meat with canned lump crab meat (but make sure it's 'lump' crab meat not the shredded variety).

Cook the pasta in a large saucepan of salted boiling water according to the packet instructions (usually about 8 minutes for al dente) – don't over cook it!

Heat a little olive oil in a frying pan/skillet over a medium heat, fry the breadcrumbs until crisp, then remove from the pan. Season with salt, pepper and a pinch of the chopped parsley and set aside.

In the same pan, add enough olive oil to cover the base of the pan and fry the diced onion for a few minutes until softened. Add the garlic, chilli/hot red pepper flakes, a few grates of lemon zest and cook for a minute before adding the brown crab meat and remaining parsley. Remove the pan from the heat.

Once the pasta is done, use a pair of tongs to pull the pasta out of the saucepan and into the frying pan/skillet and return to the heat, continue lifting the pasta in the pan until it is fully incorporated, then fold in the white crab meat and combine.

Serve in bowls with a scattering of the fried breadcrumb mixture and a pinch of salt and freshly grated black pepper on top to finish.

320 g/11½ oz. dried linguine

60 ml/¼ cup olive oil

50 g/1 cup fresh breadcrumbs

a few sprigs of flat-leaf parsley, finely chopped

1 white onion, diced

3 garlic cloves, sliced

a pinch of dried chilli/hot red pepper flakes

1 lemon

100 g/3½ oz. brown crab meat

200 g/7 oz. white crab meat

salt and freshly ground black pepper, to season

**SERVES 4**

# CREAMY SMOKED HADDOCK & MUSSEL CHOWDER

Here is my riff on cullen skink soup. Incredibly hearty, this is a meal in its own right and the epitome of comfort food. We should all be eating more mussels – they are good for the planet, good value and good for you! Serve with sliced crusty baguette.

Heat the olive oil and butter in a saucepan over a low heat and fry the onion and leeks for about 5 minutes. Season generously with salt and pepper. Once softened, add the diced potato and enough water to cover the potatoes by about 2.5 cm/1 in. Bring to a simmer, cover and cook for 10–12 minutes, until the potatoes are tender, removing the lid halfway through cooking.

Add the kale and stock/bouillon cube and continue cooking for about 6 minutes until the kale is soft, then lightly break up the potatoes with a potato masher (this helps thicken the soup without using flour). Add more water if too dry, but you want this quite thick.

While the potatoes are cooking, place the smoked haddock in another saucepan with the milk and bay leaves and simmer for about 4 minutes. Add the mussels, cover with a lid and continue cooking for a further 4 minutes until the fish is poached and cooked through. Season with cracked black pepper.

Once the fish is cooked through and the mussels are opened (if using fresh), remove the fish and pour the milk juices and mussels into the pan with the potatoes and simmer to keep warm.

Peel the skin from the smoked haddock and gently flake the fish into the soup. Fold the fish in carefully to avoid it breaking up (it's nice to have decent chunks of haddock). Garnish with chopped parsley and a squeeze of lemon juice (literally just a teaspoonful of juice), a little drizzle of olive oil and season with freshly ground black pepper. Serve with slices of baguette.

1 tablespoon olive oil, plus extra to garnish
15 g/1 tablespoon butter
1 white onion, diced
1 leek, halved lengthways and sliced and rinsed
700 g/1½ lb. potatoes peeled, cut 1-cm/½-in. cubes
100 g/3½ oz. kale or cavolo nero, stalks removed, leaves sliced
1 chicken or vegetable stock/bouillon cube
500 g/18 oz. smoked haddock fillet, undyed
500 ml/2 cups whole/full-fat milk
2 bay leaves
500 g/18 oz. mussels, fresh or pre-cooked vacuum-packed
a few sprigs of flat-leaf parsley, chopped
1 teaspoon lemon juice
sliced baguette/French stick, to serve
salt and freshly ground black pepper, to season

**SERVES 4**

# HALLOUMI BUDDHA BOWL

The secret here is to prepare the main ingredients and then source the rest from jars for a colourful weeknight meal.

Cook the beetroot/beets first. To do this, preheat the oven to 180°C fan/200°C/400°F/gas 6. Trim the stalks from the beetroot, drizzle with a little olive oil and salt generously. Wrap in foil, place on a baking sheet and cook in the preheated oven for 45 minutes. They are cooked when a skewer inserted into a beetroot passes through it with ease. Once cooked, leave to cool for 5 minutes in their foil and then peel the skin off under running water (I use a small paring knife). Season well and set aside.

While the beetroot is cooking, prepare the grain and lentil salad. Put the farro or wheat berries into a saucepan of unsalted boiling water and cook for 45 minutes, you want them tender but not mushy. Put the green lentils in a large bowl (you might actually only need half a can). Once the grains are cooked; drain them and tip into the bowl with the lentils. Whisk together the oil, vinegar and rest of the ingredients except the mint. Pour the dressing into the bowl, add the mint and fold it all together. Set aside.

Assemble each bowl ready for the warm halloumi. Grate the carrot into a small bowl and add a squeeze of lemon juice. Add a portion of the grain and lentil salad to each of four serving bowls and level the surface. Fill the bowl with clusters of the other ingredients: sliced beetroot/beets, mixed salad leaves, grated carrot, strips of roasted (bell) peppers, pickled red onions, sliced tomatoes and coriander/cilantro leaves, filling all the space to keep it looking abundant.

Heat a heavy-based griddle/grill pan to almost smoking, drizzle with a little olive oil and fry the halloumi slices for 45 seconds each side (or just long enough to colour) and add to the bowls while warm.

Drizzle each serving with a little honey and some pomegranate molasses, if using, add a sprinkle of sesame seeds and season with salt and freshly ground black pepper.

NOTE *Want to pull this together faster still? Use ready-cooked beetroot/beets and pouches of ready-to-eat lentils and/or mixed grains.*

180 g/7 oz. raw beetroot/beets (see Note)
1 large carrot
a squeeze of lemon juice
200 g/7 oz. mixed salad leaves
2 roasted red and yellow (bell) peppers from a jar, sliced into strips
pickled red onions from a jar
3 ripe vine tomatoes, thinly sliced and salted
a few sprigs each of coriander/cilantro
450 g/1 lb. halloumi
3 tablespoons runny honey
2 tablespoons pomegranate molasses (optional)
1 tablespoon sesame seeds (optional)
salt and freshly ground black pepper, to season

GRAIN & LENTIL SALAD
150 g/5½ oz. farro or wheat berries, rinsed
400-g/14-oz. can cooked green lentils, drained and rinsed
2 tablespoons olive oil
1 tablespoon cider vinegar
1 garlic clove, crushed
1 tablespoon Dijon mustard
a generous pinch of dried oregano
a handful of mint leaves, chopped

**SERVES 4**

# ALL-IN-ONE SPAGHETTI & MEATBALL TRAYBAKE

I created a version of this recipe during March 2020 when the kids and I started hosting our live cook-a-longs during the first Covid-19 lockdown. It's become a firm favourite for families around the world; I hope you enjoy it as much as we do! What makes it special is that everything is cooked in the oven from scratch (including the spaghetti from dry!).

Preheat the oven to 200°C fan/220°C/425°F/gas 7.

Break up the minced/ground meat and put it in a large bowl. Season with the smoked paprika, oregano and a pinch each of salt and pepper and add a little of the chopped parsley. Use your hands to shape into a 12 balls of equal size and set aside on a plate.

Place the dried spaghetti in a deep-sided roasting pan along with all the remaining ingredients (make sure the chicken stock is hot). Using a large fork, combine all the ingredients together and make sure the spaghetti is submerged about 1 cm/½ in. below the surface of the liquid.

Dot the meatballs on top and bake in the preheated oven for about 30 minutes. Remove from the oven and leave to rest, uncovered, for 5 minutes (don't skip this bit as it finishes the cooking process).

Sprinkle over the remaining chopped parsley, lift and drop the spaghetti with metal tongs to mix everything together and then serve.

NOTE *If the sauce seems too dry, add a splash of hot water, or if it is too loose, return it to the oven for 5 more minutes.*

400 g/1¾ cups minced/ ground beef
1 teaspoon smoked paprika
1 tablespoon dried oregano
leaves from a few sprigs of flat-leaf parsley, chopped
320 g/11½ oz. dried spaghetti
1 white onion, diced
3 garlic cloves , sliced
60 ml/¼ cup olive oil
400-g/14-oz. can cherry tomatoes, with their juice
650 ml/3 cups hot chicken stock (see page 29), or make up using stock/ bouillon cubes
1 tablespoon tomato purée/ paste
a pinch of dried chilli/hot red pepper flakes
salt and freshly ground black pepper, to season

*a deep-sided roasting pan, just big enough for a snug fit for the pasta*

SERVES 4

# BAKED SEAFOOD ORZO
# WITH LEMON DILL DRESSING

This is one of those dishes that can easily evolve from a humble dish to something more luxurious if you're entertaining or just feel like indulging yourself a little. I've kept this one quite simple for a midweek meal but feel free to upscale it! The dill dressing at the end really brings it all together. I've also cheated using pre-cooked vacuum-packed mussels from the supermarket; these are great to have in your fridge and are quick to use!

Preheat the oven to 180°C fan/200°C/400°F/gas 6.

Prepare the squid by slicing the tubes open, and score across the inside in a criss-cross pattern, then cut into bite-sized pieces or slice into rings, as preferred. Tip the pre-cooked in-shell mussels into a sieve/strainer and rinse under running water. Set both to one side.

Take an ovenproof frying pan/skillet and add enough olive oil to cover the base. Sauté the diced onion and celery for about 5 minutes, or until the onion is softened. Stir in the garlic and after 30 seconds introduce the orzo to the pan. Fry the orzo for a minute and then pour in the white wine. Continue cooking until the liquid has reduced by half, then pour in the stock followed by the petits pois, squid, mussels, tomato pureé/paste and Cajun spice. Season with salt and black pepper. Soon as the stock starts to simmer, place the whole pan, uncovered, into the oven for 15 minutes.

While the pan is in the oven, make the dressing by simply mixing all the dressing ingredients together and set aside.

After 15 minutes, remove the pan from the oven and nestle the cod loin into the orzo, scatter the sliced tomatoes over the top, drizzle with olive oil and return to the oven for a further 10 minutes.

Once the cooking time is up and the cod is cooked (see page 21), remove the pan from the oven, let rest for a minute and drizzle the dressing over the top. Place the pan in the centre of the table for everyone to serve themselves.

**200 g/7 oz. squid tubes**
**250 g/9 oz. shell-on, pre-cooked vacuum-packed mussels**
**a good splash of olive oil**
**1 large white onion, diced**
**1 celery stick/rib, finely diced**
**2 garlic cloves , sliced**
**250 g/1½ cups orzo (very small, rice-shaped pasta)**
**250 ml/1 cup white wine**
**500 ml/2 cups chicken, fish or vegetable stock (see pages 29–30), or made up with stock/bouillon cubes**
**160 g/1¼ cups frozen petits pois (no need to defrost)**
**2 tablespoons tomato purée/paste**
**1 tablespoon Cajun seasoning or smoked paprika**
**500 g/18 oz. cod loin, cut into 7.5-cm/3-in. chunks**
**6 baby plum tomatoes, halved**
**salt and freshly ground black pepper, to season**

**DRESSING**
**3 tablespoons extra virgin olive oil**
**3 tablespoons lemon juice**
**1 garlic clove, crushed**
**6 sprigs of dill, finely chopped**

**SERVES 4**

# GIFT-WRAPPED DINNER PARCELS

I used to make hundreds of these while working in the south of France and they never fail to impress! Ridiculously easy, these are great to make with kids. The bit I love is including ready-made gnocchi (in place of baby potatoes) so you literally have a meal for one ready to go. You can prep all the ingredients in advance but only assemble when you are ready to cook. Feel free to swap the fish for sliced chicken breast and leave the parcels in the oven for an extra 10 minutes.

Preheat the oven to 180°C fan/200°C/400°F/gas 6.

Prepare all the ingredients and lay the sheets of baking parchment out on a flat surface ready for assembly.

Imagine there is a small saucer placed in the centre of each piece of baking parchment – this is the area to fill with ingredients. Drizzle a little of the olive oil from the sun-dried tomatoes in this space, then divide the red onion, garlic, sun-dried tomatoes, fennel, gnocchi, courgette/zucchini and carrots between the four sheets. Finish with the tomato slices and top each one with a few torn basil leaves. Add a pinch of chilli/hot red pepper flakes and season generously with salt and pepper. Perch a cod fillet on top of each pile of assembled ingredients. Add a splash of white wine (about 3 tablespoons) and a tablespoon of butter to each stack. Season with more salt and pepper and lay a small single basil leaf on top of the fish.

Now to tie it up: bring the corners of the paper together, squeezing the excess to create a tight parcel around the ingredients. Try to ensure there are no gaps and secure the neck with the string (tying it like a shoelace).

Place the parcels on a baking sheet and bake in the preheated oven for 20 minutes. Once cooked (you should see it bubbling inside through the parchment), place each parcel in a serving bowl with a slice of charred or toasted rustic bread and a wedge of lemon.

Carefully untie the parcels and dinner is served!

12 sun-dried tomatoes in oil, sliced (reserve the oil)
1 red onion, thinly sliced
2 garlic cloves, thinly sliced
1 fennel bulb, finely sliced
500 g/18 oz. ready-made gnocchi
1 small courgette/zucchini, halved lengthways and cut into wedges
1 small carrot, peeled and thinly sliced
2 vine tomatoes, thinly sliced
leaves from a few sprigs of basil
a pinch of dried chilli/hot red pepper flakes
4 x 150-g/5½-oz. skinless and boneless cod loins or fillets
250 ml/1 cup white wine
60 g/4 tablespoons butter
salt and freshly ground black pepper, to season
4 lemon wedges
rustic bread, to serve

*4 sheets of baking parchment each about 45-cm/18-in. square*
*kitchen string/twine*

**SERVES 4**

# CREAMY FISH CRUMBLE

I do like a good fish pie, but sometimes find the traditional mashed potato topping a bit too heavy or simply don't have the time to make it, so this is when I opt for a fish crumble instead. It's a bit lighter to eat, quicker to make and I personally love the contrast between the texture of the creamy fish mixture and the crispy savoury crumble-style topping.

If you can make your own breadcrumbs I highly recommend using old sourdough and blitzing in a food processor; it creates a deliciously chewy crust; but regular breadcrumbs will work just fine too. Serve this with a lightly dressed green salad.

Preheat the oven to 180°C fan/200°C/400°F/gas 6.

Heat a splash of olive oil in a heavy-based pan set over medium heat and sauté the onion and leek for a few minutes until softened. Stir in the garlic for 30 seconds, then the curry powder, cayenne pepper and bay leaf. Add the butter to the pan along with the flour and cook for a couple of minutes. Remove the pan from the heat and whisk in the cold milk. Once incorporated, return the pan to the heat and keep whisking until the sauce thickens. Remove the bay leaf and discard.

Gently fold the fish, prawns/shrimp, petits pois and three-quarters of the chopped parsley into the sauce and simmer for a few minutes more (adding a splash more milk if it gets too thick). Spoon the fish mixture into the baking dish.

For the crumble topping, work the flour and butter together with your fingertips, then mix in the breadcrumbs, cheese and a pinch of the remaining finely chopped parsley. Season and scatter evenly over the top of the baking dish.

Bake in the preheated oven for 20 minutes, or until the top is golden and the filling is bubbling. Remove from the oven and leave to rest for about 10 minutes before serving. Scatter with any remaining chopped parsley and serve. (Take care as the sauce will be very hot.)

a splash of olive oil, for frying
1 white onion, finely diced
1 leek, sliced
1 garlic clove, chopped
1 teaspoon curry powder
a pinch of cayenne pepper
1 bay leaf
50 g/3½ tablespoons butter
50 g/heaping ⅓ cup plain/
   all-purpose flour
600 ml/2½ cups whole/full-fat
   milk
400 g/14 oz. skinless and
   boneless white fish fillets
   (total weight), cut into
   5-cm/2-in. chunks
200 g/7 oz. undyed smoked
   haddock, skinned and cut
   into 5-cm/2-in. chunks
200 g/7 oz. shelled raw prawns/
   shrimp
150 g/1 cup frozen petits pois
   (no need to defrost)
leaves from a few sprigs of
   parsley, finely chopped

CRUMBLE TOPPING
50 g/heaping ⅓ cup plain/
   all-purpose flour
25 g/2 tablespoons butter
150 g/3 cups coarse fresh
   breadcrumbs
4 tablespoons grated Parmesan
salt and freshly ground black
   pepper, to season

*2-litre/quart high-sided baking
   dish*

**SERVES 4**

# SPANISH-STYLE 'ARROZ CON COSAS'

*Arroz con cosas* translates as 'rice with things' and this is exactly that! I love nothing more than spending a couple of hours preparing and cooking a proper traditional paella on the barbecue, but sometimes you just want that paella fix without the wait! This shortcut version throws tradition out of the window and is cooked in 20 minutes, making it the perfect midweek meal. I find the bags of mixed frozen seafood are a super-convenient freezer standby when rustling this up.

Heat a little oil in a large heavy-based pan set over a high heat and sauté the onion and chicken breast for a few minutes until the chicken has coloured a little. Stir in the garlic, chipotle flakes, turmeric, smoked paprika, oregano, tomato purée/paste and season with a little salt and pepper.

Add the hot stock and stir in the rice. Mix everything together. Once it starts to bubble, add the seafood mix and the peas, give it one more stir, then cover with a lid or foil, turn the heat to medium–low and cook for about 20 minutes.

Take off the heat, remove the lid or foil and leave to rest for about 3 minutes. If it doesn't look dry enough, you can return to the heat for a few more minutes.

Finish with a drizzle of olive oil, some chopped parsley and another pinch of chipotle flakes and season with salt and pepper. Serve with the lemon wedges on the side for squeezing.

NOTE *If you don't have arborio rice, you can use any long grain white rice (including basmati) and follow the recipe as above, reducing the cooking time to 12 minutes.*

45 ml/3 tablespoons olive oil
1 white onion, diced
300 g/10½ oz. skinless, boneless chicken breast, cut into large even-sized chunks
2 garlic cloves, chopped
a pinch of chipotle chilli/chile flakes
½ teaspoon ground turmeric
1 tablespoon smoked paprika
1 tablespoon dried oregano
3 tablespoons tomato purée/paste
600 ml/2½ cups hot chicken stock (see page 29), or make up using 1½ chicken stock/bouillon cubes
320 g/1¾ cups arborio rice
350-g/12-oz. package of frozen seafood mix, defrosted
150 g/heaping 1 cup frozen petits pois (no need to defrost)
leaves from a few sprigs of flat-leaf parsley, chopped
4 lemon wedges, for squeezing
salt and freshly ground black pepper, to season

**SERVES 4**

# RELAXED
# WEEKENDS

Recipes for when you have more time

# PORK TENDERLOIN ON WHITE BEANS WITH GREMOLATA

I guarantee you all the family will love the flavours in this complete meal of pork tenderloin on a bed of creamy white beans. The herby gremolata adds a lovely freshness.

Remove the pork tenderloin from the fridge 1 hour before you are ready to cook it. Preheat the oven to 180°C fan/200°C/400°F/gas 6.

Brush the pork with the olive oil and season generously all over with salt and pepper. Heat a large ovenproof frying pan/skillet over a medium heat until hot. Place the pork in the hot pan and cook for about 3 minutes per side to brown all over. Remove the meat from the pan and set aside to rest.

Add a splash more oil to the pan the pork was cooked in (no need to clean it – you want to keep all that flavour). Add the onion and sauté for 5 minutes until softened. Stir in the garlic and cook for a minute before pouring in the white wine. Scrape the base of the pan while you simmer to reduce the wine by half.

Add the cannellini beans, paprika and chicken stock – just enough to be level with the beans – and heat for 1 minute until it bubbles. Remove from the heat and stir in any juices from the resting meat.

Place the pork loin on top of the beans, transfer the pan to the preheated oven and cook, uncovered, for 10–15 minutes. Remove, cover with foil and leave to rest for about 5 minutes.

For the gremolata, mix the parsley, garlic and lemon zest in a small bowl. Add a good pinch of salt and about 1 tablespoon olive oil – you don't want it wet, so add just enough to loosen (this isn't the traditional way, but it's how I like my gremolata!). Finish with a squeeze of lemon juice and set aside until needed.

Remove the pork loin from the pan, slice it at an angle and lay it back on top of the beans. Drizzle some olive oil around the pan, scatter a little chopped parsley over the beans and finish by spooning some of the gremolata over the pork. Serve with a sliced baguette on the side for mopping up the delicious juices.

500-g/18-oz. pork tenderloin fillet
2 tablespoons olive oil
1 large white onion, thinly sliced
2 garlic cloves, sliced
100 ml/generous ⅓ cup white wine
2 x 400-g/14-oz. cans cannellini beans, drained and rinsed
1 teaspoon smoked paprika
350 ml/1½ cups chicken stock (see page 29)
salt and freshly ground black pepper, to season
1 baguette/French stick, sliced, to serve

GREMOLATA
1 garlic clove, finely chopped
a handful of flat-leaf parsley, leaves chopped, plus extra to garnish
finely grated zest of 1 unwaxed lemon, and a squeeze of juice
about 1 tablespoon olive oil, as needed

SERVES 4

# FETA-MARINATED PORK CHOPS

Super succulent pork chops, brined first and then marinated in punchy feta that is also used as a dressing at the end. These are perfect on the barbecue, in a griddle pan or under a hot grill/broiler; buy the best quality (and biggest) pork chops you can get! I like to serve this with a salad and buttered new potatoes, or try it with the Tomatoey Bulgur Wheat on page 135.

First, make the brine. Place the salt, sugar, rosemary and lemon peel in a large mixing bowl and fill with 2 litres/quarts cold water. Stir for a few minutes to help the salt and sugar dissolve. Submerge the pork chops into the brine and leave for 1 hour. Remove the pork, rinse under cold running water to remove the brine and pat dry.

Meanwhile, make the dressing (which will also be used as your marinade). Put all the ingredients in a food processor or blender and pulverize until you have a smooth texture (the consistency of double/heavy cream). Add more water to loosen if necessary.

When you are ready to cook, pour two-thirds of the dressing into a clean bowl, cover and set aside (this is to avoid the risk of cross contamination). Pour the remaining dressing onto the pork chops and massage it in all over – the chops, not you! – and leave for 30 minutes.

Preheat the oven to 200°C fan/220°C/425°F/gas 7.

Heat a griddle/grill pan over a high heat until very hot and brush with vegetable oil. Shake off the excess feta marinade from the chops and griddle them in the hot pan for 3 minutes on each side (less if you have thinner pork chops), until charred and smoky. Do this in batches until all are cooked.

Place the griddled chops on a baking sheet and bake in the preheated oven for 5 minutes, no longer, just to crisp them up. Remove from the oven, transfer to a chopping board and leave to rest for 10 minutes.

Cut away the rib bone and slice the meat into strips at an angle. Drizzle with a little of the reserved feta dressing and add a few coriander/cilantro leaves and a wedge of lime for squeezing.

4 thick-cut pork chops (about 4 cm/½ in. thick), outside fat cut at 2.5-cm/1-in. intervals
vegetable oil, for frying
4 lime wedges, to serve

BRINE
80 g/⅓ cup salt
80 g/⅓ cup caster/granulated white sugar
a few sprigs of rosemary
peel stripped from ½ of a lemon

DRESSING/MARINADE
200 g/7 oz. feta cheese
1 fresh green chilli/chile
60 ml/¼ cup olive oil
juice of ½ a lemon
1 tablespoon cider vinegar
a pinch of salt
a handful of coriander/cilantro leaves, chopped, plus extra to garnish

**SERVES 4**

# OXTAIL STEW WITH DUMPLINGS

This is inspired by a dish I cooked on MasterChef; the secret is using dark soy sauce to create a rich umami flavour. Serve with a bowl of Perfect Mash and any green vegetable on the side.

Preheat the oven to 160°C fan/180°C/350°F/gas 4.

Season the oxtails very generously with salt and pepper. Heat a heavy-based casserole dish/Dutch oven without oil, add the oxtails and brown them all over (you may need to do this in batches) until they form a dark crust. Remove from the pan.

Reduce the heat to medium (add a splash of olive oil now if needed) and sauté the onion, leek and celery for about 5 minutes until the onion is caramelized. Add the ginger and, after 30 seconds, stir in the flour and cook for a further minute. Pour in the red wine, stirring as you do (don't worry about lumps; they'll dissolve during cooking) and simmer to reduce the liquid by half. Add all the remaining ingredients, except the coriander/cilantro, beef stock and garlic.

Cut the bunch of coriander/cilantro about halfway down, just where the leaves stop. Save the leaves to garnish, chop the stalks and add to the pot. Return the oxtails to the pot, including any juices, and pour over enough beef stock to cover. Add the halved garlic bulb and bring to the boil, cover with foil and then a tight-fitting lid (if it's not tight fitting it will dry out) and bake in the preheated oven for 5 hours (check it halfway through in case you need to add more hot water).

Meanwhile, make the dumplings. In a large mixing bowl, combine the flour and butter and lightly season with salt and pepper. Work the mixture with your fingertips until you have a scraggy mess, then add the milk and keep kneading until it all comes together; it's OK if it's a bit wet. Take a ping-pong ball-sized portion, roll in your hands to form a ball and flatten slightly, continue until all the dough is used; you'll get about 10 pieces. You can chill these until you're ready.

With 20 minutes left of cooking; remove the dish from the oven and increase the oven temperature to 180°C fan/200°C/400°F/gas 6. Place the dumplings on top of the meat/liquid (with space around each one), cover the pan again with just the lid and return to the oven for 20 minutes. Remove from the oven and leave to rest for 10 minutes before serving in bowls, garnished with coriander/cilantro.

1.5–2 kg/3¼–4½ lb. oxtail
olive oil, for frying
1 large onion, diced
1 large leek, diced
1 celery stick/rib, diced
a 5-cm/2 in. piece of ginger, cut into 1.5-cm/½-in. slices
50 g/heaping ⅓ cup plain/all-purpose flour
500 ml/2 cups red wine
1 large carrot, thickly sliced
3 star anise
2 bay leaves
60 ml/¼ cup dark soy sauce
a pinch of cayenne pepper
1 tablespoon smoked paprika
60 g/⅓ cup brown sugar
1 tablespoon white wine vinegar or cider vinegar
a small bunch of coriander/cilantro
1 litre/4 cups beef stock
1 garlic bulb, halved widthways
salt and freshly ground black pepper, to season

DUMPLINGS
200 g/1½ cups self-raising/rising flour
100 g/7 tablespoons cold butter, grated
80 ml/⅓ cup whole/full-fat milk

TO SERVE
Perfect Mash (see page 15)

SERVES 4

# CHICKEN ADOBO

This ridiculously addictive recipe is inspired by Filipino Chicken Adobo, the national dish of the Philippines. The addition of sparkling lemonade isn't exactly traditional but it does give it a sweet and sharp flavour that I enjoy. Use any brand you prefer but 'full fat' as zero sugar will not work for this. There is no chilli/chile in this recipe; instead we get the spicy 'heat' from black peppercorns, a widely used spice in the Philippines. I like to serve this with my Buttered Quinoa & Cauliflower 'Rice'.

Season the chicken thighs with the black pepper and a pinch of salt, then lightly dust with the flour. Heat the vegetable oil in a large flameproof casserole dish/Dutch oven and fry the chicken thighs skin side down for 8 minutes until the skin is golden and crisp. Turn over and cook for another few minutes, then remove from the pan.

Use a spoon to skim out any excess fat (leaving a light coating in the pan); return it to a medium–high heat and brown the onion for a few minutes. Stir in the garlic and bay leaves and, after 30 seconds (to avoid the garlic burning), pour in 250 ml/1 cup water. Continue cooking over a high heat, scraping the base of the pan to emulsify all that chicken flavour.

After a couple of minutes, stir in the soy sauce, cider vinegar, sugar and finally the lemonade. Once fully combined, return the chicken thighs to the pan, skin side up (try not to submerge the skin in the liquid and season generously with freshly ground black pepper.

Simmer for 15 minutes, or until the thighs are cooked through. Test by inserting a sharp knife into the thickest part and the juices should run clear. Remove from the heat and leave to rest for 5 minutes. If there is any excess fat from the thighs floating on the sauce, you can skim this off with a spoon and discard.

Serve the chicken adobo on top of the Buttered Quinoa & Cauliflower 'Rice', spooning over the sauce and garnish with a few sliced spring onions/scallions.

12 small chicken thighs, bone-in
1 tablespoon freshly ground black pepper
a pinch of salt
25 g/3 tablespoons plain/all-purpose flour
3 tablespoons vegetable oil
1 large white onion, sliced
5 garlic cloves, crushed
6 bay leaves
60 ml/¼ cup light soy sauce
60 ml/¼ cup cider vinegar
4 tablespoons light brown sugar
180 ml/¾ cup sparkling full-sugar lemonade
sliced spring onions/scallions, to garnish

TO SERVE
Buttered Quinoa & Cauliflower 'Rice' (see page 132)

**SERVES 4**

# POT-ROAST CHICKEN

This is total comfort food and incredibly easy; in fact this can also be made using a whole frozen chicken (see cooking times below), which I've done on a few occasions when I've forgotten to take it out of the freezer the night before! You can add whatever you like, however, for me this is about keeping it simple. I love using bunches of parsley as a proper part of the dish to eat as one of the vegetables rather than just as garnish.

Preheat the oven to 180°C fan/200°C/400°F/gas 6.

Scatter the onion wedges, potatoes, carrots, parsnips, tomatoes, thyme sprigs and bay leaves over the base of a large lidded roasting pan. Add a generous drizzle of olive oil and crumble over the stock/bouillon cube.

Place the whole chicken in the centre, nestling it in to help shift some of the vegetables to the side. Separate the parsley into smaller bunches of about four sprigs each and tuck these in just under the edge of the chicken, all the way round. Lastly squeeze in the halved garlic bulb. Pour the wine over the chicken, then add a drizzle of olive oil and the oregano and season generously with salt and pepper.

Place a small sheet of baking parchment loosely over the top of the chicken, tucking any dangling edges into the sides of the pot, then on with the lid and into the preheated oven for 1 hour (if cooking the chicken from frozen, cook for 1½ hours).

Remove the pan from the oven, along with the lid and parchment (be careful of the steam), baste the chicken with the juices from the pan and return to the oven, uncovered, for 30 minutes until the chicken is golden or the juices run clear when a knife is inserted in to the thickest part of the thigh. Cover the chicken and leave to rest for 10 minutes before serving.

Carve the chicken, placing slices of it into serving bowls along with the vegetables and bunches of parsley. Finish by spooning a generous amount of the cooking liquid into each bowl, add a quick squeeze of lemon, a little drizzle of olive oil and a pinch of salt.

1 large red onion, cut into 2.5-cm/1-in. wedges
250 g/9 oz. new potatoes, any larger ones halved
3 carrots, halved lengthways and sliced at an angle
2 parsnips, halved lengthways and sliced at an angle
2 vine tomatoes, roughly chopped
a few sprigs of thyme
2 bay leaves
a generous drizzle of olive oil
1 chicken stock/bouillon cube
1.3-kg/2¾-lb. chicken
a large bunch of flat-leaf parsley
1 garlic bulb, halved widthways
250 ml/1 cup rosé or white wine
1 teaspoon dried oregano
1 lemon, halved, for squeezing
sea salt and freshly ground black pepper, to season

30-cm/12-in. enamel roasting pan with lid, or similar

**SERVES 4**

# PORCHETTA WITH ANCHOVIES

The Italian word porchetta translates to 'little pig' but in this instance we are using good-quality pork belly filled with an aromatic stuffing, full of salty flavour from anchovies. I sometimes swap the anchovies for 2–3 tablespoons of 'nduja (spicy spreadable salami). (See photograph on pages 84–85.)

Preheat the oven to 220°C fan/240°C/450°F/gas 8.

In a bowl, mix together the anchovies, rosemary, sage, parsley, garlic, chilli/hot red pepper flakes, olive oil and a pinch of salt and pepper and set aside.

Prepare the pork belly. Score the skin of the pork belly in a criss-cross fashion, then turn it over and butterfly the meat – to do this place the meat on a flat surface, then use a very sharp knife running parallel to the work surface to slice through the middle of the meat so it opens like a book – this isn't vital but does give you more surface area to season and stuff. With the skin-side down and meat facing you spread the anchovy and herb mixture over the meat. Roll it up and tie with butchers' string/twine. The easiest way is to tie it individually (so cut 5–6 x 45.5-cm/18-in. lengths of string) and simply tie it around the rolled meat to hold it in place.

Keeping the skin dry, season the meat with salt and pepper and then place in a large ovenproof dish or roasting pan. Roast in the preheated oven for 10 minutes before turning the temperature down to 160°C fan/180°C/350°F/gas 4 and leave to cook for 4 hours.

Meanwhile, boil the new potatoes for about 12 minutes in a saucepan of salted boiling water. Add the carrots to the pan halfway through the cooking time. Drain, then drop the potatoes and carrots into a mixing bowl with the red onions and halved garlic bulb (if using), coat with a little olive oil and salt. Scatter these around the porchetta about 30 minutes before the end of the cooking time.

Once the porchetta is done, remove it from the oven and let rest for at least 30 minutes. Serve the porchetta whole on a carving board with the roasted carrots, potatoes, garlic bulb and red onions to the side.

6 anchovy fillets, chopped

leaves stripped from 1 sprig of rosemary, chopped

leaves stripped from 1 sprig of sage, finely chopped

a handful of flat-leaf parsley, chopped

4 garlic cloves, peeled and crushed

a pinch of dried chilli/hot red pepper flakes

2 tablespoons olive oil, plus extra for coating

2-kg/4½-lb. pork belly

1 kg/2¼ lb. new potatoes

450 g/1 lb. heritage carrots, scrubbed

2 large red onions, quartered

1 garlic bulb, halved widthways (optional)

sea salt and freshly ground black pepper, to season

*butchers' string/twine*
*large ovenproof dish or*
*    roasting pan*

**SERVES 4–6**

# MARMALADE-GLAZED BAKED SALMON

I love the bittersweet taste of this marmalade glaze – its zingy citrusy flavour pairs so well with rich, oily fish like salmon. This is best served on a whole salmon side to slice at the table. Try it with my Black Rice Tabbouleh and/or Green Vegetable Medley. (See photograph on pages 88-89.)

Remove the side of salmon from the fridge 30 minutes before you are ready to cook it. Preheat the oven to 200°C fan/220°C/425°F/gas 7.

Drizzle a little olive oil onto a large flat baking sheet, season the skin of the salmon with a teaspoon of sea salt, then lay it, skin-side down, on the baking sheet.

Mix all the marmelade glaze ingredients together. Taste and adjust, adding more honey or vinegar to get a nice sharp/sweet flavour. Spoon just enough of the glaze to generously cover the salmon side and spread it all over. Bake, uncovered, in the preheated oven for 10 minutes.

Remove the salmon from the oven and spoon over the remaining glaze. Use the back of the spoon to delicately smother the salmon, ensuring you don't wipe away the existing glaze. Return the salmon to the oven to bake for a further 10 minutes.

Once cooked, carefully transfer the salmon to a large serving plate, garnish with snipped chives and lemon wedges (for squeezing) and cut into slices to serve.

1-kg/2¼-lb. side of salmon
olive oil, for drizzling
1 teaspoon sea salt flakes
snipped chives
lemon wedges, to serve

MARMELADE GLAZE
200 g/1⅔ cups marmalade, smooth or fine shred
2 tablespoons runny honey
1 tablespoon cider vinegar
juice of ½ a lemon
1 garlic clove, crushed
½ teaspoon sea salt
1 teaspoon freshly ground black pepper
leaves stripped from a sprig of thyme

TO SERVE
Black Rice Tabbouleh (see page 139)
Green Vegetable Medley (see page 18)

SERVES 6–8

# DUCK PROVENÇAL
# WITH PUY LENTILS

This meal cleverly uses one tray to roast the veg, crisp up the duck and warm the lentils. If you like, serve with little cubes of crispy roast potatoes which, although they need a separate baking sheet, can be added to the oven 30–45 minutes before the duck is ready. Enjoy with dollops of Dijon mustard.

Preheat the oven to 180°C fan/200°C/400°F/gas 6.

Add the onion, leek, carrots, tomatoes, caraway seeds, herbes de Provence, vinegar, pinch of salt and drizzle of olive oil to a deep-sided roasting pan. Rub a little olive oil into the duck portions and season generously with salt and pepper. Place them on top of the vegetables and roast in the preheated oven for 1 hour.

Remove the pan from the oven and transfer the duck portions to a plate. Lift the pan slightly, spoon out any excess oil and discard. Gently fold the Puy lentils into the vegetables in the pan. Return the duck portions to their previous position on top of the vegetables and return the whole thing to the oven to cook for a further 30 minutes.

Meanwhile, get the Crispy Cubed Potatoes ready to cook – you can add them to the second shelf in your oven 30–45 minutes before the duck finishes cooking. Leave the skin on and roughly cut them into 1.5-cm/½-in. cubes. Put the olive oil in a bowl, tip in the cubed potatoes and add a pinch of salt. Toss with your hands to coat them with oil. Tip onto a baking sheet and roast in the oven for 30–45 minutes at the same temperature as the duck, shaking the baking sheet halfway through cooking. Season with salt and herbes de Provence once cooked.

Garnish the duck with parsley and serve with the potatoes on the side.

1 red onion, sliced
1 large leek, halved lengthways, sliced and rinsed
2 carrots, halved lengthways and sliced
400-g/14-oz. can cherry tomatoes with their juice
1 tablespoon caraway seeds
1 tablespoon dried herbes de Provence
1 teaspoon cider vinegar
2 tablespoons olive oil
4 duck thighs and leg joints (about 225 g/8 oz. each)
250-g/9-oz. pouch of cooked Puy lentils
2 garlic cloves, crushed
freshly chopped flat-leaf parsley, to garnish
sea salt and freshly ground black pepper, to season
Dijon mustard, to serve (optional)

CRISPY CUBED POTATOES
1½ tablespoons olive oil
1 kg/2¼ lb. floury potatoes
a pinch of salt
a few pinches of dried herbes de Provence

*a deep-sided roasting pan*
*a baking sheet*

**SERVES 4**

# COOLBOX SOUS VIDE RACK OF LAMB

When I first started as a private chef I used to use my coolbox as a makeshift 'sous vide' or waterbath. I've cooked hundreds of racks of lamb using this method and it never fails – give it a go!

Remove the lamb from the fridge an hour before you want to start cooking. Add half the olive oil and a sprig each of rosemary and thyme to each ziplock bag. Season the lamb and place one rack in each bag. Massage the olive oil around the lamb. Fill a large bowl with water and slowly submerge each open bag into the water – this forces the air out of the bag. Once all the air pockets are gone, zip up the bags.

Fill the cool box with hot water from the kettle to roughly the depth of the bags. The water need to be 55°C/130°F, so use a thermometer to measure the temperature, and add cold water to adjust it.

Carefully lower in the bags, leaving the zip above the waterline, but ensuring the meat is fully submerged and there are no air pockets. Cover the coolbox with its lid. Check the temperature every 30 minutes, topping up with more hot water as needed to keep it at 55°C/130°F. Leave for at least 1 hour (or up to 3 hours).

Lift the bags from the water and place on a tray. Open each bag carefully and pour the meat juices into a saucepan set over a medium heat. Bring to the boil, then remove from the heat. Pass through a fine sieve/strainer, discard the solids and reserve the stock.

Remove the lamb from the bags, pat dry and season. Brown in a hot frying pan/skillet with a little olive oil, half the butter, the garlic and the remaining sprigs of herbs. Remove the lamb from the pan and set aside. Pour in the red wine and simmer until reduced by two-thirds. Add the reserved stock, increase the heat and keep cooking on a rolling boil until reduced by half again. Turn the heat to low, whisk in the blackcurrant jam/jelly and remaining butter and simmer until glossy. Pass the jus through a sieve/strainer to remove all the herbs. If you want a thicker sauce; simply mix together 1 teaspoon cornflour/cornstarch and 1 tablespoon of cold water and pour into the sauce and warm through to thicken.

Slice the racks of lamb into four (allowing about two ribs per slice) and serve 2 portions per person. Serve with Roasted Cracked New Potatoes with Rosemary, any green vegetable and the red wine jus.

2 racks of lamb, French trimmed and fat removed
2 tablespoons olive oil
4 sprigs of rosemary
4 sprigs of thyme
50 g/3½ tablespoons butter
1 garlic bulb, halved widthways
250 ml/1 cup red wine
2 tablespoons blackcurrant jam/jelly
1 teaspoon cornflour/cornstarch (optional)
sea salt and freshly ground black pepper, to season

TO SERVE
**Roasted Cracked New Potatoes with Rosemary (see page 17)**

*2 large ziplock bags*
*a coolbox/ice chest*
*a digital food thermometer*

**SERVES 4**

# PIQUANT CHICKEN CASSEROLE

This rustic chicken dish is a bit of a hybrid, inspired by simple French cooking techniques but with the headline flavours of a Greek stifado; that is to say sharp vinegar tempered with butter for a lip-smacking sauce. Serve with minted mini roast potatoes and a green salad drizzled with olive oil and vinegar.

Preheat the oven to 160°C fan/180°C/350°F/gas 4.

Boil the new potatoes for 10 minutes in a saucepan of salted water, then drain. Return to the saucepan with the olive oil and season generously with salt and pepper. Toss to coat with the oil and tip onto a baking sheet and cook on the top shelf of the preheated oven for 30–40 minutes, or until they've turned slightly golden. Once cooked, remove from the oven, return the potatoes to the saucepan with a little butter and stir until the butter has melted and the potatoes are coated. Finish with a pinch of salt and the mint and set aside until the chicken is ready.

Meanwhile, make a start on the chicken. Lightly dust the chicken portions in the flour (just a very light dusting!) and season with salt and pepper. Heat a large shallow casserole dish/Dutch oven with a splash of vegetable oil and fry the chicken legs and thighs, skin-side down, for about 8 minutes, or until the skin is golden, turning the legs throughout. Turn over the thighs and cook for a further 5 minutes. Remove the chicken from the pan and pour away any excess fat.

In the same pan, add some olive oil and fry the onions, bay leaves and thyme for a few minutes, then stir in the butter and vinegar and simmer for a minute. Stir in the garlic and tomatoes and return the chicken to the pan (including any collected juices), ensuring the thighs are skin-side up. Pour in the wine, bring back to a simmer, season generously with salt and pepper, cover with a lid and bake in the oven for 35 minutes, removing the lid for the final 5 minutes.

Once cooked, remove from the oven and taste; you want it buttery with a slight sharpness from the vinegar; add more butter or vinegar to get the balance right and then garnish with chopped parsley. Serve with the roasted new potatoes and a dressed green leaf salad.

8 chicken portions
  (thighs and legs)
2 tablespoons plain/all-purpose
  flour
a splash of vegetable oil
a splash of olive oil
2 large red onions, halved,
  cut into 2.5-cm/1-in. wedges
2 bay leaves
a few sprigs of thyme
50 g/3½ tablespoons butter
2 tablespoons white wine
  vinegar
3 garlic cloves, peeled and
  sliced into thirds lengthways
4 vine tomatoes, cut into
  chunks
150 ml/⅔ cup white wine
a few sprigs of flat-leaf parsley,
  roughly chopped
sea salt and freshly ground
  black pepper, to season

MINTED BABY ROASTIES
750 g/1 lb. 10 oz. baby new
  potatoes, any larger ones
  halved
2 tablespoons olive oil
20 g/1½ tablespoons butter
a handful of mint leaves, finely
  chopped, or a pinch of
  dried mint

*a large lidded casserole dish/
Dutch oven*

SERVES 4

# SPANAKOPITA PARCELS
# WITH TOMATO & CHICKPEA RAGÙ

These feta- and ricotta-filled pastries are inspired by a Greek classic and will bring a little Aegean sunshine to your table. Serve with a tomato and chickpea ragù for a complete meal.

Preheat the oven to 180°C fan/200°C/400°F/Gas 6.

For the spanakopita, drain the canned spinach, pushing it into a sieve/strainer to remove as much liquid as possible and discard the liquid. Place the spinach in a mixing bowl along with the feta, ricotta, nutmeg, dill, egg and spring onions/scallions. Fold everything together until fully incorporated but don't overwork it; it's nice to have a few chunks of feta.

Lay a sheet of filo/phyllo out flat on the work surface/counter. Brush with melted butter and lay another sheet on top. If they are quite big, cut them in half (you only want them to be about the size of a sheet of writing paper). Place a spoonful of the filling in the centre (about the size of an egg), wipe a circle of melted butter onto the pastry around the filling and pull the sides of the pastry up to create a mini wonton-type parcel. Gently pinch the edges together to make a parcel. Place on a baking sheet lined with baking parchment. Continue until all the parcels are made. Bake in the preheated oven for 30 minutes, then remove and let cool for 5 minutes before serving.

For the tomato and chickpea ragù, fill the base of a frying pan/skillet with the olive oil and gently fry the garlic for a couple of minutes over a low heat. Before the garlic starts to colour, stir in the halved baby plum tomatoes, turn the heat up to medium and leave to simmer for 5 minutes; you can push down on some of the tomatoes with a spatula/potato masher to help release their juices. If it starts to get too dry, add 1–2 tablespoons water. Add a pinch of sugar, a generous pinch of salt and lots of black pepper to give it a kick and stir in the chickpeas. Continue cooking for another 5 minutes until the chickpeas are warmed through and the sauce is thickened and emulsified. Remove from the heat.

Serve the spanakopita parcels with a spoonful or two of the tomato and chickpea ragù with a simple green salad on the side.

400-g/14-oz. canned or frozen spinach (not fresh)
200 g/7 oz. feta cheese, crumbled
100 g/½ cup ricotta
freshly grated nutmeg, to taste
6 sprigs of dill, snipped
1 egg
2 spring onions/scallions, finely sliced
12 sheets filo/phyllo pastry
100 g/1 stick minus 1 tablespoon butter, melted

TOMATO & CHICKPEA RAGÙ
60 ml/¼ cup olive oil
2 garlic cloves, sliced
250 g/9 oz. baby plum tomatoes, halved
a pinch of caster/granulated sugar
500 g/18 oz. cooked chickpeas/garbanzo beans, drained and rinsed (I prefer the plump ones in a jar, but you could use canned)
freshly chopped flat-leaf parsley, to garnish
salt and freshly ground black pepper, to season

SERVES 4–6

# CUBAN-STYLE BRISKET WITH ORANGE SALSA

Good things come to those who wait… such as beef brisket slow-cooked with lashings of rum, served with rice and beans cooked in the meat juices and a punchy fresh orange salsa.

Remove the brisket from the fridge at least 30 minutes before you are ready to cook it. Preheat the oven to 220°C fan/240°C/465°F/gas 8.

Season the brisket generously with salt and pepper. Heat a large frying pan/skillet until smoking hot, add a splash of vegetable oil and cook the brisket for about 10 minutes, until browned all over. Transfer to a deep-sided roasting pan or casserole dish/Dutch oven.

Return the pan to medium heat, add a splash of olive oil and sauté the onions for 2 minutes. Add the garlic and chilli/chile and pour in the rum – this may flame up so stand back and let it cook out. Stir in the tomato purée/paste, cumin, paprika, bay leaves and oregano and crumble in the stock/bouillon cube. Add 500 ml/2 cups just-boiled water, bring to a simmer and then pour the liquid over the brisket.

Lay a sheet of baking parchment over the brisket, followed by a tight-fitting piece of foil and top with a lid. Place in the preheated oven, reduce the temperature to 150°C fan/170°C/325°F/gas 3 and cook for 6–8 hours. Remove from the oven and leave to rest for 30 minutes with the lid on. Once rested, reserve the cooking liquor and shred the meat with two forks, then use a pair of kitchen scissors or a knife to chop it further; return the meat to the pan, cover and set aside.

To make the orange salsa, place the spring onions/scallions, parsley, coriander/cilantro, garlic, salt, olive oil, baby plum tomatoes and lemon and orange juices, then drop the spent orange half into the food processor (yes, the entire thing! But no pips). Add 2 tablespoons water and pulse until you have a smooth purée.

To make the rice, measure the rice in a cup or jug/pitcher, tip into a saucepan and stir in the beans. Using the same measure you used for the rice, add double the volume of brisket cooking liquor. Mix together, bring to a simmer, cover, reduce the heat to low and leave to cook for 12 minutes, then fluff with a fork.

Plate the brisket with the rice and garnish with coriander/cilantro. Serve with the orange salsa, hot sauce and lime wedges for squeezing.

1-kg/2¼-lb. beef brisket, tied
vegetable oil, for frying
olive oil, for frying
2 white onions, sliced
3 garlic cloves, chopped
1 fresh green jalapeño chilli/
    chile, chopped
100 ml/scant ½ cup dark rum
2 tablespoons tomato purée/
    paste
1 tablespoon ground cumin
1 tablespoon paprika
2 bay leaves
2 tablespoons dried oregano
1 chicken stock/bouillon cube
about 250 g/1⅓ cups basmati
    rice (see recipe method)
400-g/14-oz. can black beans,
    drained and rinsed
salt and freshly ground black
    pepper, to season

ORANGE SALSA
3 spring onions/scallions
10 g/⅓ oz. flat-leaf parsley
10 g/⅓ oz. coriander/cilantro
3 garlic cloves, peeled
1 teaspoon salt
45 ml/3 tablespoons olive oil
12 baby plum tomatoes
juice of ½ lemon
½ an orange

TO SERVE
sprigs of coriander/cilantro
hot sauce of your choice
lime wedges

*a deep-sided roasting pan or
    casserole dish/Dutch oven*

**SERVES 4**

# FAMILY FAKEAWAYS

Homemade takeaway classics

# FISH & CHIPS WITH MUSHY PEAS & CURRY SAUCE

A great British classic; nothing beats a proper fish supper with mushy marrowfat peas and chip-shop curry sauce! Part of the secret to creating perfectly crispy fish is to double fry it; which might seem like more work, but actually makes serving dinner much easier as you can prep all the elements a little in advance and then finish off and plate it all up while it's still hot.

Put the cod fillets on a plate and liberally sprinkle with the salt. Cover and leave for 30 minutes. When time is up, briefly rinse under cold water and pat dry with paper towels and set aside.

To make the batter, put the flour, cornflour/cornstarch, vinegar, baking powder, turmeric and a pinch of salt in a bowl. Whisk in enough sparkling water to create a smooth batter with a cream-like consistency. Set aside until needed.

Heat the vegetable oil in a heavy-based saucepan or deep fat fryer to about 180°C/350°F, or until a pinch of flour sizzles in seconds.

Put the flour on a plate and season with salt and pepper. Dust the fish fillets in the seasoned flour and shake off any excess. Next dip them into the batter to fully coat, then gently place them in the hot oil, using metal tongs. Cook for 5 minutes, then remove and place on a wire rack. Don't discard the oil – you will be frying the fillets a second time just for a minute before serving (this makes them extra crispy!)

To make the chips/fries, cut the potatoes into thick chips the full length of the potato and about 1 cm/½ in. thick; you can leave the skin on. Heat the oil in a heavy-based pan until medium hot. Fry the chips for 8 minutes, or until light golden; this stage cooks the chips but they won't be very crispy. Remove them with a slotted spoon onto paper towels and set aside. Just before serving, turn the heat up on the oil so it's very hot and refry the chips for a minute until deep golden and crisp. Remove again with slotted spoon and season with salt.

4 cod fillets
  (about 200 g/7 oz. each)
1 tablespoon salt
500 ml/2 cups vegetable oil,
  for deep frying
200 g/1½ cups plain/
  all-purpose flour
salt and ground white pepper,
  to season

BATTER
130 g/1 cup plain/all-purpose
  flour
50 g/½ cup cornflour/
  cornstarch
1 tablespoon malt vinegar
1 teaspoon baking powder
a pinch of ground turmeric
a pinch of salt
250 ml/1 cup sparkling water

CHIPS/FRIES
1 kg/2¼ lb. floury baking
  potatoes (see Top Tips for
  Perfect Chips, page 17)
500 ml/2 cups vegetable oil,
  for deep frying (you can use
  the same oil you cooked the
  fish in, if liked)
65 g/½ cup plain/all-purpose
  flour
sea salt flakes and cayenne
  pepper, to season

*Recipe continued on following page.*

For the curry sauce, heat the oil in a frying pan/skillet set over a medium heat. Add the onion and sauté for 5 minutes until soft and slightly caramelized. Stir in the garlic and cook for 30 seconds, then add the turmeric, curry powder, soy sauce, sugar, salt and stock. In a cup, mix together the cornflour/cornstarch with 1 tablespoon cold water and stir into the sauce to thicken. Taste, adding more salt or sugar as needed. Once thickened, remove from the heat and transfer to a serving bowl or small jug/pitcher ready to serve.

For the mushy peas, pour the entire contents of the can of marrowfat peas into a small saucepan with the butter, cayenne pepper and Worcestershire sauce. Set over a low heat and bring to a simmer. Lightly squash the peas with a potato masher to thicken, season generously with black pepper and stir in the vinegar. Remove from the heat and transfer to a serving bowl.

When you are ready to eat, refry the chips in their original reheated oil for another couple of minutes, then place in a bowl and season with salt and cayenne. Refry the fish fillets for another minute to crisp them up, then place onto a paper towels to drain of the excess oil and season with salt. Serve everything together while it is hot and enjoy!

## A FEW TIPS ON THICKENING SAUCES

If you want to thicken any sauce or a stew you can always add a cornflour/cornstarch slurry; mix together equal quantities of cornflour/cornstarch (a tablespoon is usually enough for a litre/quart of liquid) and COLD water, then stir it into what you want to thicken and continue to stir as you warm it through. But be warned – if you cook at too high a temperature for too long the starch can breakdown and the sauce can go runny again.

Another cheat my brother-in-law Ciro taught me years ago is to mix butter or oil with equal quantity of plain/all-purpose flour, again about a tablespoon of each for a litre/quart of liquid, until you have a paste and then drop this into any sauce you want to thicken, stirring as you do. Mixing the plain/all-purpose flour with oil or butter first means it won't form lumps in your sauce and is a more stable thickening agent.

### CURRY SAUCE

**2 tablespoons olive oil**
**1 small white onion, finely diced**
**1 garlic clove, crushed**
**½ teaspoon ground turmeric**
**1 tablespoon mild curry powder**
**1 tablespoon soy sauce**
**a pinch each of sugar and salt**
**300 ml/1¼ cups chicken or vegetable stock (see page 29), or make using stock/bouillon cubes**
**1 tablespoon cornflour/ cornstarch**

### MUSHY PEAS

**300-g/10½-oz. can marrowfat processed peas (undrained), or use dried green split peas, cooked**
**1 tablespoon butter**
**a pinch of cayenne pepper**
**½ teaspoon Worcestershire sauce**
**1 teaspoon cider vinegar**
**freshly ground black pepper, to season**

**SERVES 4**

# CHICKEN KORMA

So I stole this recipe from my mum who regularly made it for us as we were growing up – we couldn't get enough of it! I can't say how authentic it is... but I can guarantee it's delicious. Serve with rice and/or naan bread on its own or as part of a spread with the recipes on pages 108 and 109. (See photograph on pages 106–107.)

Mix the grated fresh ginger with the yogurt in a large mixing bowl. Add the cubed chicken, cover and leave to marinate in the fridge for at least 1 hour, or preferably overnight – although I have been known to dunk and cook straight away if I've got a hankering for this curry!

Add the onions, garlic and 2 tablespoons water into a spice blender or food processor and pulse to a paste. If you don't have access to a food processor chop everything as finely as possible by hand.

When you are ready to cook, heat the vegetable oil in a heavy-based lidded frying pan/skillet set over a low heat and fry the whole spices for 30 seconds, then stir in the onion and garlic paste. Leave this to cook, stirring occasionally, for 10 minutes, then finally stir in the ground spices. Turn the heat up to medium and add the marinated chicken, still coated in yogurt, to the pan and fry the chicken for 10 minutes, turning occasionally.

Add the coconut milk, ground almonds, salt and sugar and top up with 100 ml/scant ½ cup water. Bring to a simmer, cover with the lid and leave to cook for 30 minutes. Remove the lid after 15 minutes to reduce and thicken the sauce, stirring occasionally to stop it catching. If you want it thicker, or leave on the hob/stovetop for a little longer to reduce.

Once cooked, remove from the heat, squeeze in the juice of half a lime and let rest for 5 minutes. Garnish with coriander/cilantro leaves and toasted almonds and serve on rice with lime wedges for squeezing.

You can enjoy this on its own with rice and/or naan breads and any of the other curry dishes on pages 108–109.

a 5-cm/2-in. piece of fresh ginger, grated
200 g/scant 1 cup natural/plain Greek-style yogurt
600 g/21 oz. boneless and skinless chicken breasts, cut into 5-cm/2-in. cubes
2 white onions, roughly chopped
4 garlic cloves, peeled
2 tablespoons vegetable oil
400 ml/1⅔ cups coconut milk
100 g/1 cup ground almonds
1 teaspoon salt
1 tablespoon demerara/turbinado sugar
2 limes, 1 quartered, 1 halved
freshly chopped coriander/cilantro, to garnish
2 tablespoons toasted flaked/slivered almonds

WHOLE SPICES
2 x 10-cm/4-in. cinnamon sticks
6 cloves
2 bay leaves
2 whole dried chillies/chiles

GROUND SPICES
1 teaspoon ground turmeric
1 teaspoon ground cumin
1 tablespoon ground coriander
1 tablespoon garam masala
1 tablespoon mild curry powder
a few grinds of black pepper

TO SERVE
basmati rice (see page 12)
lime wedges

**SERVES 4**

# CLASSIC CHICKEN CURRY

There's nothing quite like a reliable curry recipe and this doesn't take as long as the list of ingredients suggests! You can swap the chicken for fish, simply place large chunks of skinless and boneless white fish on top of the sauce 5 minutes before the end of cooking time. (See photograph on page 107.)

Heat the vegetable oil in a heavy-based lidded frying pan/skillet set over a low–medium heat. Add the whole spices and toast for 1 minute. Add the onions and cook for 8 minutes, stirring occasionally, until golden. Stir in the garlic, ginger, tomato purée/paste, chilli/chile, salt and sliced tomatoes and add about 60 ml/¼ cup water. Cover with the lid and leave to simmer for 5 minutes.

Remove the lid, stir in the ground spices, and fold in the chicken cubes. Pour in the chicken stock, cover again and let simmer gently, for a further 8 minutes.

Remove the lid again and leave to simmer over a slightly higher heat (you want it to be bubbling) for 8 minutes, or until the sauce has reduced and thickened (see Note below).

Remove from the heat, squeeze in the juice of half a lime and let rest for 5 minutes before garnishing with chopped coriander/cilantro.

Serve with the reserved onion and tomato slices, lime quarters for squeezing and yogurt dusted with a little ground cumin.

You can enjoy this on its own with basmati rice and/or naan breads and any or all of the other curry dishes on pages 105 and 109.

NOTE *If you want a thicker sauce, either leave to simmer for longer or mix 1 heaped tablespoon cornflour/cornstarch with cold water (same quantity as the cornflour) and stir into the curry. Heat gently and it should thicken while being stirred.*

2 tablespoons vegetable oil
2 red onions, thinly sliced
    (reserve a few to serve)
3 garlic cloves, crushed
a 5-cm/2-in. piece of fresh
    ginger, grated
1 tablespoon tomato purée/
    paste
1 fresh red chilli/chile,
    finely chopped
1 teaspoon salt
400 g/14 oz. tomatoes, thinly
    sliced (reserve a few to serve)
600 g/21 oz. skinless and
    boneless chicken breast,
    cut into 5-cm/2-in. cubes
300 ml/1¼ cups chicken stock
    (see page 29), or made using
    stock/bouillon cubes
2 limes, 1 halved, 1 quartered
freshly chopped coriander/
    cilantro, to garnish
natural/plain Greek-style
    yogurt, to serve

WHOLE SPICES
2 x 10-cm/4-in. cinnamon sticks
1 tablespoon coriander seeds
3 star anise
6 cardamom pods
12 curry leaves
2 dried whole chillies/chiles

GROUND SPICES
1 teaspoon ground turmeric
1 tablespoon ground cumin
1 tablespoon ground coriander
1 tablespoon garam masala
1 teaspoon curry powder
1 teaspoon sugar
1 teaspoon chilli/chili powder

**SERVES 4**

# SAAG PANEER

Marinated paneer crispy fried and smothered with an aromatic spinach sauce is the perfect accompaniment to any fakeaway curry dish. I like to use canned spinach for convenience and to keep it cost effective; using fresh spinach would require a huge amount of spinach and work! (See photograph on pages 106–107.)

Place the paneer cubes in a bowl and add the ground turmeric, paprika and chilli/chili powder. Mix together until the paneer is fully coated in spices.

Heat the vegetable oil in a pan over a high heat, add the paneer cubes and cook for a few minutes without moving them. Turn the cubes over to brown the other side; once golden all over, remove from the pan and put on a plate lined with paper towels.

To make the spinach sauce, take the same pan and add a splash of vegetable oil. Add the onions and sauté for 5 minutes, until a deep caramel colour. Stir in the garlic and chilli/chile and cook for another minute before adding the turmeric, cumin, cumin seeds, garam masala and salt. Cook for 30 seconds, stirring all the time.

Stir in the spinach and heat through; you may need to add a splash of water to loosen it. Once it's warm, stir in the butter and cream and fold in the fried paneer cubes. Once the paneer has heated through, remove the pan from the heat and finish with a squeeze of lime juice, a swirl of cream and a scattering of nigella seeds (if using).

You can enjoy this on its own with basmati rice and/or naan breads and any or all of the other curry dishes on pages 105–108.

PANEER
**500 g/18 oz. paneer, cut into 2.5-cm/1-in. cubes**
**1 teaspoon ground turmeric**
**1 tablespoon paprika**
**1 teaspoon chilli/chili powder**
**1 tablespoon vegetable oil**

SPINACH
**a splash of vegetable oil**
**2 white onions, diced**
**2 garlic cloves, sliced**
**1 fresh green chilli/chile, finely chopped**
**1 teaspoon ground turmeric**
**1 tablespoon ground cumin**
**1 teaspoon cumin seeds**
**1 tablespoon garam masala**
**1 teaspoon salt**
**2 x 400-g/14-oz. cans cooked spinach, drained**
**30 g/2 tablespoons butter**
**100 ml/scant ½ cup double/ heavy cream, plus extra to serve**
**lime wedges, for squeezing**
**nigella/onion seeds, to garnish (optional)**

**SERVES 4**

# TRAY-BAKED BURGERS IN BUNS

I love game-changing recipes like this one. We love burgers in our house and my tray-baked version, where everything is cooked from scratch, makes pulling together an affordable burger dinner for the whole family a cinch! (You might like to also check out my Crispy Cauliflower Steak Burgers on page 38.)

Take the minced/ground meat out of the fridge 15 minutes before you are ready to start cooking. Preheat the oven to 200°C fan/220°C/425°F/gas 7.

Put the meat in a bowl with the oregano, onion, Cajun seasoning and salt. Use your hands to bring it all together but don't overwork it – you want a fairly loose mixture. Divide the mixture into 4 portions of equal size and form into patties just under 1 cm/½ in. thick and the same diameter as your burger buns.

Place the bottom half of the buns into a tight-fitting baking pan, top with a slice of Cheddar cheese, then add the meat patty followed by a slice of mozzarella, then spread your sticky condiment on the top half of the bun and place on top of the burger. Brush the top of the bun with a little melted butter and add a sprinkle of salt.

Tightly cover the baking pan with foil and bake in the preheated oven for 30 minutes. Remove the pan from the oven and let the burgers rest for 5 minutes with the foil on. Remove the foil, check the meat is cooked and serve!

NOTE *Depending on your oven, how cold the ground meat is and how thick your patties are, cooking times may vary slightly. Always check the burgers are cooked through before serving.*

400 g/14 oz. minced/ground beef
2 tablespoons dried oregano
1 white onion, grated
1 tablespoon Cajun seasoning or smoked paprika
1 teaspoon salt
4 brioche burger buns, split
4 slices of Cheddar cheese (not processed burger cheese slices, they will turn into a melted mess!)
4 slices of firm mozzarella cheese
a sticky condiment of your choice (caramelized onions, bbq sauce or tomato ketchup)
20 g/1½ tablespoons butter, melted

*a high-sided baking pan*

**SERVES 4**

# HOMEMADE FLATBREAD 'PIZZA'

This is far from a traditional pizza recipe but easy and tasty too! There are endless different toppings you could choose, but I've shared my favourites here to get you started.

Preheat the oven to 220°C fan/240°C/465°F/gas 8.

To make the dough, mix the flour, yogurt, salt and olive oil together in a bowl and, once it starts to bind, tip out onto a floured worksurface/counter and knead until it forms a soft dough. Add more flour or yogurt if too wet or dry. Cover with a damp kitchen towel and let rest for 10 minutes.

Mix all the sauce ingredients together in a bowl and set aside.

Divide the dough into 4 pieces of equal size and roll out to a thickness of about 1 cm/½ in. that is roughly the diameter of your pan/skillet. Heat the pan on the hob/stovetop over a medium heat and place the disk of dough in the pan. Cook for a couple of minutes. While it's cooking, spread some of the sauce over the surface. Scatter over cheese to cover, then add whatever toppings you like – but do not be tempted to overload!

After the pan has been over the heat for a few minutes, transfer it to the preheated oven to cook for 6–8 minutes, until the cheese is bubbling and the toppings are hot.

Slide it out of the pan onto a board and use a pizza cutter or large knife to slice and serve just as you would a pizza!

### SUNBLUSHED TOMATO & BASIL
Scatter a handful of sunblushed tomatoes over the pizza, bake as above, then garnish with small basil leaves just before serving.

### RED ONION, ANCHOVY & ROCKET
Sprinkle thinly sliced red onion over the pizza and dot with anchovy fillets. Bake as above, then scatter over rocket/arugula dressed with olive oil and balsamic vinegar.

### MOZZARELLA, 'NDUJA & BLACK OLIVE
Add a thin layer of grated cheese then add a sliced mozzarella ball (or mini mozzarella balls) and dot with marble-sized pieces of 'nduja (spicy spreadable salami) and a few sliced pitted black olives.

**about 250 g/2¾ cups 50/50 mix of grated Cheddar and firm mozzarella cheese**

FLATBREAD DOUGH
**300 g/2 cups self-raising/rising flour, plus extra for dusting**
**300 g/1 cup natural/plain yogurt (not Greek-style)**
**a pinch of salt**
**1 tablespoon olive oil**

SAUCE
**300 g/1¼ cups tomato passata (sieved/strained Italian tomatoes)**
**1 tablespoon dried oregano**
**1 tablespoon tomato purée/paste**
**½ teaspoon sea salt flakes**
**1 tablespoon runny honey**

*a large ovenproof frying pan/skillet*

**SERVES 4**

# FRIED CHICKEN BUCKET

Homemade fried chicken just like you get in a bucket! I prefer to joint a whole chicken to get a variety of pieces but you can simply buy chicken pieces from the supermarket if you prefer.

For the fried chicken, put the egg and milk in a large mixing bowl and whisk in the cayenne, paprika, turmeric and dried herbs. Add the chicken and make sure it is all submerged. Cover and leave to marinate in the fridge for at least 1 hour, or preferably overnight.

Preheat the oven to 180°C fan/200°C/400°F/gas 6.

Mix the flour and cornflour together in a separate large bowl.

When you are ready to start cooking, heat the vegetable oil in a large heavy-based pan until it starts to shimmer. Shake off the excess marinade from the chicken pieces and drop them in the bowl of flour to coat. Fry the chicken pieces in the hot oil for 8 minutes, turning halfway through cooking. Place the chicken pieces on a wire rack set on a baking sheet (you may have to do this in batches) and then transfer to the preheated oven to bake for 40 minutes, or until the juices run clear when pierced with a knife.

As soon as the chicken comes out of the oven, season generously with salt flakes and let cool for 5 minutes.

To make the corn-on-the-cob, mix the butter, salt, nigella seeds (if using) and paprika together in a bowl. Lay 4 sheets of foil open, place a cob of corn on top of each one and brush all over with the butter. Wrap the foil around the cobs and bake in the preheated oven at 180°C fan/200°C/400°F/gas 6 for 30 minutes.

To make the BBQ baked beans, simply place the beans in a saucepan with the bbq sauce and paprika. Heat over a medium heat until warmed through, then transfer to a bowl ready to serve.

Serve the hot crispy fried chicken and all the sides together, along with plenty of paper napkins and cold drinks.

### FRIED CHICKEN
**1 egg (any size)**
**500 ml/2 cups whole/full-fat milk**
**1 tablespoon cayenne pepper**
**1 tablespoon paprika**
**1 tablespoon ground turmeric**
**2 tablespoons dried mixed herbs**
**1 chicken, jointed (drumsticks, thighs, wings, breasts)**
**290 g/2 cups plain/all-purpose flour**
**100g/1 cup cornflour/cornstarch**
**500 ml/2 cups vegetable oil, for deep frying**
**1 tablespoon sea salt flakes**

### CORN-ON-THE-COB
**70 g/5 tablespoons butter**
**a pinch of salt**
**1 tablespoon nigella/onion seeds (optional)**
**a pinch of smoked paprika**
**2 cobs of sweetcorn/corn, halved widthways**

### BBQ BAKED BEANS
**400-g/14-oz. can baked beans in tomato sauce**
**2 tablespoons bbq sauce**
**1 tablespoon smoked paprika**

### CHIPS/FRIES (OPTIONAL)
**Great Chips/Fries (see page 16)**

*a wire rack set over a baking sheet*

**SERVES 4**

# CRISPY CHILLI BEEF

This Chinese-inspired recipe always reminds me of my mum; as a kid, every time we used to order a takeaway this was her go-to dish! So here you go mum... this one's for you x.

Put all the ingredients for the sauce in a bowl, add 60 ml/¼ cup water and mix to combine. Set aside.

Place clingfilm/plastic wrap over the steaks and lightly bash them with a rolling pin (or base of a saucepan) – this tenderizes the meat and will also make for much thinner strips. Pop the steaks in the freezer for 15 minutes to firm up slightly and make them easier to slice thinly.

Slice the steaks against the grain (widthways) into thin strips, 3 mm/ ⅛ in. thick and lightly dust in the Chinese five spice.

Place with cornflour/cornstarch in a mixing bowl. Break the eggs into a separate bowl and beat them.

Drop the steak strips into the cornflour/cornstarch to coat, then shake off any excess flour and dip into beaten egg. Shake off any excess and place them back in the cornflour/cornstarch (they will clump together but keep shaking them about and they will separate).

Heat the oil in a large, heavy-based saucepan until shimmering. Carefully fry the steak strips for 3 minutes, or until crisp (you might need to do this in batches). Remove from the oil using a slotted spoon and place on a plate lined with paper towels. Set the pan aside but don't discard the oil. Once all the steak strips have been fried and left to cool for 5 minutes, reheat the oil and, once shimmering, fry the steak strips for a second time for 1 minute – this double-fry creates extra crispy strips! Transfer to a plate lined with clean paper towels.

Heat a splash of oil in a clean frying pan/skillet set over a high heat. Sauté the ginger, garlic, chilli/chile and springs onions/scallions for a minute – don't let them burn. Pour in the sauce; it will start bubbling immediately. After 30 seconds, or just as the sauce starts to thicken, throw in the crispy beef strips and stir just to coat them in the sauce, then remove from the pan straightaway and put into a serving dish. Garnish with snipped chives and some slices of red chilli/chile and serve with plenty of basmati rice.

600 g/21 oz. rump steak
1 teaspoon Chinese five spice
300 g/3 cups cornflour/
    cornstarch
2 eggs
250 ml/1 cup vegetable oil,
    for frying
a 5-cm/2-in. piece of fresh
    ginger, chopped
3 garlic cloves, chopped
1 fresh red jalapeño chilli/chile,
    finely diced, plus extra slices
    to garnish
6 spring onions/scallions,
    cut into 5-cm/2-in. lengths
snipped chives, to garnish
basmati rice, to serve
    (see page 12)

SAUCE
45 ml/3 tablespoons cider
    vinegar
45 ml/3 tablespoons runny
    honey
60 ml/¼ cup tomato ketchup
45 ml/3 tablespoons sweet
    chilli/chili sauce
15 ml/1 tablespoon dark soy
    sauce
a pinch of salt

**SERVES 4**

# CHINESE ORANGE CHICKEN

In America there is a Panda Express Chinese Kitchen on almost every street corner. When I lived there, I always headed straight for their orange chicken when a takeaway craving kicked in.

Line up three mixing bowls. Mix both the flours and Chinese five spice together in one bowl. Beat the eggs in the second bowl and place the cubed chicken in the third bowl.

Heat the vegetable oil in a heavy-based frying pan/skillet set over a medium heat. Check it is hot enough by dropping in a pinch of flour; if it sizzles immediately, the oil is ready.

When you are ready to cook, coat the chicken cubes in the flour, then dip into the beaten egg and then back into the flour. Carefully drop the coated chicken into the hot oil (you might need to do this in batches) and cook for 6 minutes, or until golden, turning over halfway through cooking time if not fully submerged. Use a slotted spoon to remove from the oil and place on a plate lined with paper towels. Set the pan aside but don't discard the oil.

To make the sauce, mix the cornflour/cornstarch with 1 tablespoon cold water and set aside. Zest 1 of the oranges and set aside. Heat the oil in a frying pan/skillet set over a very high heat. Stir-fry the red and green (bell) peppers and red onion for 1 minute, then transfer to a plate and reduce the heat to low.

Once the pan has cooled slightly, sauté the garlic, ginger and chilli/chile for 30 seconds. Squeeze in the juice of both oranges and add the soy sauce, sesame oil and sugar. Keep stirring until it just bubbles, then immediately remove from the heat and stir in the vinegar, 200 ml/¾ cup water and the cornflour/cornstarch slurry. Return the pan to the heat and stir continuously until the sauce is thick and glossy. Reduce the heat to low and stir in the reserved orange zest, peppers and red onion. If it's too thick, add a splash more water.

Set the pan with the oil back over heat, and once shimmering, add the chicken and cook for 1 minute; this double-fry will make them extra crispy! Remove from the oil with a slotted spoon onto a plate lined with clean paper towels and season with salt. Stir the crispy chicken into the orange sauce, garnish with a sprinkle of nigella seeds and a few spring onions/scallions and serve with rice.

50 g/½ cup cornflour/cornstarch

130g/1 cup plain/all-purpose flour

1 teaspoon Chinese five spice

2 eggs

3 skinless and boneless chicken breasts, cut into 1.5-cm/½-in. cubes

400 ml/1⅔ cups vegetable oil, for deep frying

2 spring onions/scallions, thinly sliced on the angle

a pinch of onion/nigella seeds

basmati rice, to serve (see page 12)

ORANGE SAUCE

1 tablespoon cornflour/cornstarch

2 oranges

1 tablespoon vegetable oil

1 red (bell) pepper, cut into chunks

1 green (bell) pepper, cut into chunks

1 red onion, halved and cut into 2.5-cm/1-in. slices

3 garlic cloves, sliced

a 5-cm/2-in. piece of fresh ginger, grated

1 fresh red chilli/chile, chopped

2 tablespoons soy sauce

1 tablespoon sesame oil

80 g/⅓ cup plus 1 tablespoon light brown sugar

1 tablespoon cider vinegar

**SERVES 4**

# CHICKEN GYROS

A proper gyro can be made with chicken, pork or lamb; this one has chicken thighs wrapped in a soft pillowy Greek-style pita bread and is served with tzatziki plus tomato and cucumber.

Mix all the marinade ingredients together in a large bowl. Score the chicken thighs through the skin with three cuts made into the flesh, then add them to the marinade. Cover and leave to marinate in the fridge for at least 1 hour, or preferably overnight.

For the tzatziki, simply mix all the ingredients together in a bowl. Taste, adding more mint or salt as needed. Cover and chill until needed. For the garnish, prepare the tomatoes, cucumber, red onion and parsley, place in separate bowls and set aside.

Take the chicken out of the fridge 30 minutes before you want to cook it to bring to room temperature.

Preheat the grill/broiler to as hot as possible.

Wipe away any excess marinade from the chicken thighs and place them skin-side up under the grill/broiler. Cook for about 12 minutes, or until the skin is crisp and charred in places, checking it frequently. Once they look done, turn them over and cook the other side for 5 minutes, or until cooked through. Transfer to a dish to rest while you get everything else together.

When you are ready to serve, thinly slice the chicken widthways, pop into a warm dish and pour over any collected juices.

Splash the pita breads with a little water and toast under the grill/broiler for a minute just to warm them through.

Swipe a spoonful of tzatziki across the warmed pita bread, top with slices of chicken, tomatoes, cucumber, red onion, chopped parsley, a good squeeze of lemon juice and a pinch of salt. Roll the gyro as tightly as you can and take a humungous bite! Serve with some hot oregano-dusted chips/fries on the side if you fancy them, or you can even stuff them inside the pita bread too.

6 chicken thighs, skin-on and deboned
8 soft Greek-style pita breads

MARINADE
100 g/½ cup plain/natural yogurt Greek-style
juice and grated zest of ½ a lemon
2 tablespoons olive oil
1 tablespoon smoked paprika
1 tablespoon ground cumin
½ teaspoon cayenne pepper
2 garlic cloves, crushed
1 tablespoon dried oregano

TZATZIKI
250 g/1 cup plain/natural Greek-style yogurt
1 garlic clove, crushed
leaves from 6 sprigs of mint, finely chopped
1 tablespoon olive oil
½ teaspoon salt
juice of ½ lemon
¼ cucumber, grated, juice squeezed out

TO SERVE
2 vine tomatoes, diced
½ a cucumber, diced
1 red onion, finely diced
a handful of freshly chopped flat-leaf parsley leaves
lemon wedges, for squeezing
Great Chips/Fries (see page 16), dusted with dried oregano (optional)

**SERVES 4**

# SALADS & SIDES

Great tasting salads & side dishes

# ROASTED BEETROOT, CARROT, FETA, WALNUTS & HONEY

This warm salad of earthy vegetables with feta, walnuts and honey has become very popular in our household. It's perfect served as a side dish during the winter months, or as a hearty addition to any meal in the summer. I wear gloves to peel my beetroot/beets to avoid my fingers being pink for a week!

Preheat the oven to 180°C fan/200°C/400°F/gas 6.

Blanch the carrots in a saucepan of boiling water for 5 minutes, then drain and leave to steam dry for a couple of minutes. Transfer them to a roasting pan and add the thyme sprigs and red onion wedges.

To prepare the beetroot/beets, cut the stalks off and rinse them, roughly chop and add to the roasting pan. Slice the beetroots into 5-cm/2-in. wedges. Add them to the carrots and stalks in the roasting pan and toss to mix all the vegetables together. (You want your roasting pan to be a snug fit for the vegetables so they are slightly piled up with no gaps inbetween them.)

Drizzle over the oil and vinegar, sprinkle with the cumin seeds and season generously with salt and pepper. Bake, uncovered, in the preheated oven for about 45 minutes, or until a skewer can be passed through a beetroot/beet wedge with a little resistance.

Remove from the oven and immediately fold in the walnuts, feta and chopped parsley. Drizzle with the honey while the vegetables are all still warm and serve.

300 g/10½ oz. carrots, cut into 5-cm/2-in. pieces, thicker ones halved lengthways
a few sprigs of thyme
2 red onions, halved and cut into 2.5-cm/1-in. wedges
500 g/18 oz. raw beetroot/beet
2 tablespoons olive oil
1 tablespoon balsamic vinegar
1 tablespoon cumin seeds
100 g/¾ cup walnut halves
200 g/7 oz. feta
a few sprigs of flat-leaf parsley, chopped
generous 1 tablespoon runny honey
salt and freshly ground black pepper, to season

**SERVES 4 AS A SIDE**

# SWEET CHILLI, MANGO & ROCKET SALAD

I could eat this on its own, but it works well as a side dish with most grilled fish and meat dishes, adding a little summer sunshine. Juicy ripe mango fruit is nicer, not to mention cheaper, than buying chunks in a tub so I've give you clear instructions on how to handle it, but obviously if it's a bridge too far, buy it ready cubed!

If you want to turn this into a more substantial salad to serve as a main meal, add strips of poached or grilled chicken breast.

Peel and finely slice the onion, put in a dish of cold water with a few ice cubes and set to one side; this will crisp the slices up and make them milder to eat.

To make the mango cubes, hold the mango on its side so one of the pointed ends is facing you. Slice downwards using a sharp serrated knife to remove one of the 'cheeks', guiding the blade around the stone/pit. Turn the mango around and repeat on the other side, holding the mango with a thick tea towel/dish cloth to protect your fingers. Using the tip of the knife, score the flesh in a diagonal pattern along the length of the mango, but try to avoid cutting through any skin. Next, turn the mango 90 degrees and score again to make a criss-cross pattern. Turn the scored mango side over and use your fingers to push on the skin so the fleshy side pops out! The scored mango chunks will separate and stick out so you can cut them away from the skin using a paring knife. Alternatively, rather than cubes, you can slice the flesh into strips.

Add the mango to a large mixing bowl. Drain the onion, pat dry with paper towels and add to the bowl. Add the rocket/arugula and mint.

To make the dressing, place all the ingredients in a small bowl and whisk (or place in a screwtop jar and shake vigorously) until combined. Pour over the mango salad, toss to coat everything in the dressing and transfer to a serving dish. Serve fairly quickly or the leaves will go soggy.

1 small red onion
1 large or 2 small ripe mangoes (you want about 500 g/18 oz. prepared flesh)
50 g/1¾ oz. cups rocket/arugula (or a bag of mixed baby salad leaves)
leaves from a few sprigs of mint, torn

SWEET CHILLI/CHILE DRESSING
1 small garlic clove, crushed
1 tablespoon light brown sugar
1 red chilli/chile, flesh finely chopped (leave the seeds in for extra heat)
juice of ½ a lime
a pinch of salt
½ tablespoon fish sauce
1 tablespoon olive oil
1 teaspoon cider vinegar

**SERVES 4 AS A SIDE**

# LETTUCE 'STEAKS' WITH HALLOUMI CROÛTONS

These are great fun for the kids and a nice alternative to the usual green salad bowl. Thick-cut wedges of lettuce are topped with a creamy mayo-style dressing and served with a generous sprinkle of crispy halloumi croûtons. You can store any leftover dressing in an airtight jar in the fridge for 3 days.

Make the dressing first: crack the egg into a hand-blender cup or bowl with the rest of the dressing ingredients and process with a hand blender for a few minutes until fully emulsified. Transfer to a bowl, cover and set aside until needed.

Heat a frying pan/skillet until very hot, then drizzle in a little olive oil. Add the halloumi, shaking the pan to spread them out and fry for 30 seconds (or until they start to colour). Add the garlic and dried chilli/hot red pepper flakes, if using. Shake the pan to colour the other side of the halloumi cubes for another 30 seconds. Transfer to a bowl and stir in the chopped parsley and mint.

Trim the very end of the iceberg stalks for a clean cut, then remove any loose outer leaves. Slice 2.5-cm/1-in. thick 'steaks', cutting through the stalk so they hold together. Lay the lettuce on a serving dish.

Liberally spoon the dressing over the 'steaks', top with the warm halloumi croûtons and serve.

**2 iceberg/crisphead lettuces**

CREAMY DRESSING
**1 large/extra-large egg**
**1 tablespoon cider vinegar**
**1 tablespoon Dijon mustard**
**250 ml/1 cup vegetable oil**
**a pinch of paprika**
**freshly ground black pepper**

HALLOUMI CROÛTONS
**2 tablespoons olive oil**
**200-g/7-oz. block of halloumi, cut into 1-cm/½-in. cubes**
**1 garlic clove, finely chopped**
**a pinch of dried chilli/hot red pepper flakes (optional)**
**leaves from a few sprigs of parsley and mint, chopped**

**SERVES 4 AS A SIDE**

# TRAY-BAKED ASPARAGUS GREENS

Try this simple one-pan recipe for green vegetables roasted with a splash of rosé wine and butter and you won't be disappointed! Perfect served with simply cooked chicken breast or fish or try it with my Marmalade-glazed Baked Salmon (see page 87).

Preheat the oven to 200°C fan/220°C/425°F/gas 7.

Place the green beans, garlic, wine, butter and a splash of olive oil in a deep-sided roasting pan. Toss to mix everything together and season generously with salt and pepper. Bake, uncovered, in the preheated oven for 8 minutes, then remove from the oven but don't turn the oven off.

Fold in the asparagus spears, petits pois and tarragon, giving the pan a good shake to help combine the wine and butter. Return the pan to the oven to cook for a further 8 minutes.

Remove from the oven and immediately fold in the baby spinach, ensuring everything is coated in the buttery juices. Squeeze the lemon over the whole lot and gently mix it all together.

Transfer to a shallow serving dish, discarding any leftover liquid. Serve immediately.

100 g/3½ oz. fine green (French) beans, trimmed
2 garlic cloves, sliced
125 ml/½ cup dry rosé or white wine
85 g/¾ stick butter, cubed
a splash of olive oil
500 g/18 oz. fresh asparagus spears, woody ends trimmed
100 g/⅔ cup frozen or fresh petits pois or peas
leaves from a sprig of tarragon
a large handful of baby leaf spinach or other robust green salad leaves
1 lemon, halved
salt and freshly ground black pepper, to season

**SERVES 4 AS A SIDE**

# BUTTERED QUINOA & CAULIFLOWER 'RICE'

Frozen cauliflower rice is not something I enjoy but freshly pulverized cauliflower mixed with quinoa to add a nutty note is delicious. It needs a good whack of butter, and to be seasoned generously, but is a good way to squeeze some veg into the family's diet and the quinoa is full of protein too so it's win win. This is particularly delicious with the Chicken Adobo on page 81.

Put the quinoa in a sieve/strainer and rinse under running water. Tip it into a large saucepan of simmering water and cook for about 12–15 minutes, or until the grains are chewy but not crunchy. Tip back into the sieve/strainer to drain, and then return to the saucepan. Cover with a lid (or plate) until needed.

Remove the stalk and leaves from the cauliflower and break it into florets. Place the florets in a food processor. Chop any tender leaves and the stalk by hand and add these to the food processor. Pulse until you have a 'rice'-type consistency.

Heat the butter with a splash of olive oil in a very hot frying pan/skillet and stir in the cauliflower 'rice'. Stir-fry for a few minutes just to heat it through, then add the cooked quinoa and stir to combine. Season with a generous pinch of salt. Remove from the heat and serve.

TIP *To ring the changes, you can add different dried spices (smoked paprika, a pinch of curry powder, ground turmeric) to the pan with the butter and oil, or stir in finely chopped green herbs, such as coriander/cilantro or flat-leaf parsley at the end of the cooking time.*

**100 g/½ cup dried red quinoa (or use a combo of red and white if that's what you've got)**
**1 large cauliflower**
**50 g/3½ tablespoons butter**
**2 tablespoons olive oil**
**salt**

**SERVES 4 AS A SIDE**

# TOMATOEY BULGUR WHEAT

This is an extremely versatile side dish of bulgur wheat – one of my go-to store-cupboard heroes. I've kept this version quite simple so that it will go with everything, but I often add lots of chopped fresh herbs to give it a little more kick, or you can add a jar of rinsed chickpeas/garbanzo beans to make it more filling. Try it with the Feta-Marinated Pork Chops (see page 77) as feta and tomato always get on well together.

Heat the olive oil in a large lidded frying pan/skillet set over a medium heat. Add the onion and sauté for 5 minutes until softened and slightly caramelized.

Stir in the tomato purée/paste, diced tomato and stock cube and then add the bulgur wheat. Top up with hot water (it should only just enough to cover the surface of the bulgur wheat).

Bring to the boil, then cover and reduce the heat to a gentle simmer. Cook for 10 minutes. Remove from the heat and let stand, still covered, for a further 10 minutes. Once time is up, remove the lid, fluff up the grains with a fork, stir in your choice of herbs and season generously with salt and pepper.

Serve warm or at room temperature.

2 tablespoons olive oil
1 white onion, finely diced
1 tablespoon tomato purée/ paste
1 large ripe vine tomato, diced
1 chicken or vegetable stock/ bouillon cube
150 g/scant 1 cup coarse grain bulgur wheat, rinsed
about 300 ml/1¼ cups hot water (see method)
your choice of soft green herbs, such as coriander/ cilantro, flat-leaf parsley, basil, finely chopped
salt and freshly ground black pepper, to season

**SERVES 4 AS A SIDE**

# VILLAGE SALAD

I've called this a village salad as it reminds me of the salads my Greek Cypriot family make, with lots of herbs and a bit of crunch from shredded white cabbage. Even though it features feta, this isn't to be confused with a Greek salad. Freestyle the salad as much as you want, adding other salad veg or herbs to suit your preference. You can also leave out the feta and serve it with the Spanakopita Parcels on page 97, in place of the Tomato & Chickpea Ragù) for a lighter meal.

Peel and finely slice the onions, put in a dish of cold water with a few ice cubes and set to one side; this will crisp the slices up and make them milder to eat.

Meanwhile, prepare the rest of the salad vegetables as follows, dropping them into a large salad bowl as you go.

Shred the lettuce and cabbage. Deseed and thinly slice the (bell) pepper. Half the cucumber lengthways and drag a teaspoon along the seeds to scoop them out and discard. Slice the cucumber flesh widthways to create little crescents. Halve the tomatoes. Drain the onion slices, pat them dry with paper towels and add them to the salad bowl. Add the olives, fresh herbs and oregano. Break the feta into bite-sized chunks and add to the bowl with all the salad vegetables – they will break down further as you mix the salad.

Combine the dressing ingredients in a small bowl and whisk until cloudy and emulsified (or place in a screwtop jar and shake vigorously). Pour over the salad and use two large spoons or salad servers to toss everything together to coat the salad in little pieces of tangy feta.

Transfer the salad into a large serving bowl and serve immediately.

½ a small red onion
1 small cos/romaine lettuce
¼ a white cabbage
½ a green (bell) pepper
½ a large cucumber
12 baby plum tomatoes, halved
100 g/1 cup kalamata olives, stoned/pitted and halved
a handful of dill, torn
a handful of flat-leaf parsley leaves, torn
a handful of coriander/cilantro leaves, torn
a handful of mint leaves, torn
2 tablespoons dried oregano
200 g/7 oz. feta cheese

DRESSING
60 ml/¼ cup olive oil
60 ml/¼ cup red wine vinegar
a few grinds of black pepper
a pinch of salt

**SERVES 6 AS A SIDE**

# BLACK RICE TABBOULEH

This delicious side is inspired by Middle Eastern-style grain salads, such as tabbouleh, and is packed with fresh herbs and crunchy pomegranate and pumpkin seeds/pepitas. The chewy texture of the black rice contrasts nicely with fish dishes – try it with the Marmalade-glazed Baked Salmon (see page 87), or use as the base for a meal by simply topping with some oven-roasted vegetables and/or slices of pan-fried halloumi (see page 61).

Bring a large saucepan of water to the boil, add the black rice and simmer, uncovered, for about 25 minutes, or according to the packet instructions, until cooked.

While the rice is cooking, put the chopped sundried tomatoes, oil from the jar of tomatoes, red onion, balsamic vinegar and tomato purée/paste in a large mixing bowl with a pinch of salt. Mix to combine. Stir in the pomegranate seeds and pumpkin seeds/pepitas and add the chopped herbs.

Once the rice is cooked, drain and while it is still in the sieve/strainer rinse briefly under cold running water.

Tip into the mixing bowl with the rest of the ingredients. Fold in the baby spinach leaves in batches and then taste, adding more olive oil, balsamic vinegar and salt, as needed. Transfer to a serving dish and enjoy.

250 g/1⅓ cups black rice
80 g/3 oz. sundried tomatoes in olive oil, roughly chopped
45 ml/3 tablespoons olive oil from the jar of sundried tomatoes
1 red onion, very finely diced
2 tablespoons balsamic vinegar
2 tablespoons tomato purée/paste
100 g/½ cup pomegranate seeds
2 tablespoons pumpkin seeds
20 g/¾ oz. flat-leaf parsley, chopped (you will need quite a lot!)
leaves from a few sprigs of mint, chopped
a large handful of baby spinach leaves, roughly sliced
salt

**SERVES 4 AS A SIDE**

# SWEET THINGS

Tempting treats & desserts

# BANANA PANCAKE LOVE LETTERS

These crispy fried banana-filled pancakes drizzled with condensed milk and dusted with spiced sugar are a popular street-food snack throughout South-east Asia, and never fail to satisfy. They are so popular in fact, that the backpacking route is often referred to as the Banana Pancake Trail. I've eaten more of these than my waistline cares to remember... You can enjoy them for a weekend brunch, or they make a great dessert.

To make the pancake dough, put the flour and salt in a bowl and mix together. Add 125 ml/½ cup water and mix until you have soft dough-like consistency (add more water if it is too dry or more flour if it is too wet). Pull off small amounts of dough and use your hands to roll them into golf-ball-size portions. Put on a tray, cover with a damp cloth or clingfilm/plastic wrap and leave to rest for about 15 minutes.

Mix the ground cinnamon, cayenne pepper and sugar together in a small bowl and set aside.

When you are ready to cook, flatten a ball of dough and use a rolling pin to roll it out as thinly as you can in a fairly even square shape. Lightly dust a piece of baking parchment with flour and lay the dough square on top. Place some banana slices in the centre, leaving a gap all the way around it, then immediately fold over the edges to make an envelope. Repeat with the remaining dough and banana slices.

Heat a large frying pan/skillet set over a medium heat and add a knob/pat of butter. Pick up the parchment paper with the filled dough on it and with your hand under the parchment flip this carefully into the pan, peeling away the parchment. Cook for a few minutes, or until golden and crisp, then add another small knob of butter to the pan, flip the pancake over and fry for another 2 minutes until golden. Remove from the pan onto a plate and cover with foil to keep warm while you cook the rest of the pancakes.

Slide the pancakes onto serving plates, drizzle with condensed milk and sprinkle with the spiced sugar mix. Serve warm.

150 g/1 cup plain/all-purpose flour, plus extra for dusting
½ teaspoon salt
1 teaspoon ground cinnamon
a pinch of cayenne pepper
35 g/3 tablespoons white granulated sugar
2 ripe bananas, cut into 5-mm/¼-in. slices
50 g/3½ tablespoons butter
canned condensed milk, to serve

**MAKES 4**

# PUFFED PANCAKE CUPS WITH BLACKCURRANT COMPOTE & CUSTARD

This is fun! My puffed pancake cups are really sweet Yorkshire puddings/popovers. Slightly sweet, filled with a speedy custard cream and topped with blackcurrant compote, these are good enough to have for breakfast, brunch or dessert! I've tried all three options, several times... Feel free to swap the blackcurrants for any other fruit you like – blueberries come a close second.

Preheat the oven to 210°C fan/230°C/450°F/gas 8.

Start with the compote. Place the blackcurrants (keeping a few back), sugar and lemon juice in a saucepan and add 2 tablespoons water. Gently cook over a medium heat for 12 minutes, stirring frequently, until the blackcurrants have broken down and turned into a sauce. Drop in the remaining blackcurrants and continue cooking for another 5 minutes to warm them through. Transfer to a bowl and set aside.

To make the custard cream, whisk the cream, icing/confectioners' sugar and vanilla extract together in a mixing bowl until you have soft but firm peaks. Pour the custard into the bowl and whisk a third of the whipped cream into the custard. Fold in the rest, cover and chill in the fridge until needed.

To make the pancake cups, put about 1 tablespoon vegetable oil into each hole in the cupcake pan. Place in the preheated oven for 10 minutes to heat up.

Whisk all the batter ingredients together in a large bowl and pour into a jug/pitcher. Carefully remove the cupcake pan from the oven and immediately pour enough batter to fill each hole halfway, then immediately return to the oven for 15 minutes (don't open the door during cooking!). Once done, remove the fluffy pancake cups from the oven and leave to cool for 30 minutes (they will fall a little).

Once they are cooled and you are ready to serve, simply spoon the custard cream into the middle followed by some of the blackcurrant compote. Finish with a little dusting of icing/confectioners' sugar and serve.

vegetable oil, for baking

COMPOTE
**300 g/3 cups frozen blackcurrants**
**80 g/½ cup plus 1 tablespoon granulated sugar**
**1 teaspoon lemon juice**

CUSTARD CREAM
**150 ml/⅔ cup double/heavy cream**
**1 tablespoon icing/confectioners' sugar, plus extra for dusting**
**½ teaspoon vanilla extract**
**400-g/14-oz. can/carton ready-made custard**

BATTER
**350 ml/1½ cups whole/full-fat milk**
**200 g/1½ cups plain/all-purpose flour**
**3 UK large/US extra-large eggs**
**½ teaspoon ground cinnamon**
**1 teaspoon vanilla extract**
**a pinch of salt**

*12-hole cupcake or muffin pan*

**MAKES 12**

# LEMON & THYME MERINGUE PIE

A twist on the beloved classic... The homemade curd is delicious in its own right – I keep any leftovers in a jar and stir it into Greek yogurt, use it to fill a cake or just spread it on my toast!

Make the pastry case/pie shell following the recipe on page 31.

After baking the pastry, reduce the oven temperature to 160°C fan/180°C/350°F/gas 4.

To make the lemon and thyme curd, separate the egg yolks from the whitesinto two separate bowls. Beat the egg yolks. Place the cornflour/cornstarch, thyme leaves, sugar and 300 ml/1¼ cups cold water in a saucepan and heat over a medium heat, whisking continuously – it will turn into a thick paste in seconds. Remove from the heat.

Add a tablespoon of the paste to the beaten egg yolks in a bowl and whisk. Continue this process – tempering the egg yolks – until you've used at least half of the paste. Then transfer the egg yolk mixture into the saucepan (off the heat) with the remaining paste and whisk until fully incorporated. Return the saucepan to the heat and whisk in the lemon juice, zest, a pinch of salt and the butter. Continue whisking at a leisurely pace for about 3 minutes, or until the mixture starts to bubble (be careful, it will be very hot). Remove from the heat – you now have a gorgeous lemon and thyme curd.

To make the meringue, whisk the egg whites until they turn opaque, then add the cornflour/cornstarch, cream of tartar and vanilla extract. Keep whisking until soft peaks start to form, then add half the sugar and whisk. Once incorporated, whisk in the remaining sugar until you get firm peaks and immediately stop. You don't want to overwhisk it.

Fill the cooled pastry base/pie shell with the curd and level the surface with the back of a spoon. Add spoonfuls of the meringue to cover the surface of the curd, ensuring it touches the pastry case/tart shell edge; this helps 'anchor' the meringue. Use the back of the spoon to create peaks and make the meringue look pretty.

Bake in the preheated over for 20 minutes or until the meringue is lightly golden. Leave to cool in the tin/pan for 30 minutes before slicing to serve.

1 x Shortcrust Pastry Tart Case/
Pie Shell (see page 31)*,
or use a store-bought one
if you are short of time

LEMON & THYME CURD
4 egg yolks
60 g/heaping ½ cup cornflour/
cornstarch
½ teaspoon thyme leaves
150 g/¾ cup caster/white
granulated sugar
4 lemons, juice and finely
grated zest
a pinch of salt
40 g/3 tablespoons butter

MERINGUE
4 egg whites
1 tablespoon cornflour/
cornstarch
a pinch of cream of tartar
½ teaspoon vanilla extract
100 g/½ cup caster/superfine
sugar

*25-cm/10-in. tart tin/pan*

**SERVES 6–8**

* You can make the Shortcrust
Pastry Case/Pie Shell up to
3 days in advance

# CHERRY SHERBET MOUSSE

A cherry sherbet is a thing of beauty; a real celebration of the fruit. The mousse aspect gives this a light and fluffy texture and is much more robust than making an ice cream or sorbet. You can of course make this in advance and pop into the freezer (or just make it and serve!). The recipe works equally well with any sweet frozen fruit; peaches and blueberries work nicely.

Place the cream, icing/confectioners' sugar and almond extract in a mixing bowl. Stir gently at first to incorporate the sugar, then use an electric whisk to whisk until you have soft, stable peaks. Cover and chill in the fridge until needed.

Chop 12 cherries by hand and set aside. Add the remaining frozen cherries to a blender with the caster/superfine sugar, salt, kirsch (if using) and lemon juice and pulse until you have a smooth purée/paste. You can pass the cherry pulp through a sieve/strainer to remove the skins if preferred (simply push the pulp through with the back of a spoon) or leave as it is if you want the added texture. Stir the reserved chopped cherries into the pulp.

Add a third of the whipped cream to the cherry pulp and mix together. Gently fold in the rest of the whipped cream until it's almost all incorporated – it's quite nice to have it not totally combined and leave it with a slightly marbled effect.

Either serve immediately in little glass tumblers or pour into a freezerproof container and freeze until ready to use. If freezing, remove from the freezer 5 minutes before serving.

**NOTE** *If you decide to freeze the sherbet, warming an ice cream scoop in a cup of boiling water first will help to scoop it out more easily.*

300 ml/1¼ cups double/ heavy cream, chilled

3 tablespoons icing/ confectioners' sugar

1 teaspoon almond extract

800 g/4 cups frozen stoned/ pitted sweet cherries

200 g/1 cup caster/superfine sugar

a pinch of salt

1 tablespoon kirsch or brandy (optional)

½ teaspoon fresh lemon juice

**SERVES 4–6**

# POACHED PEARS WITH ORANGE BLOSSOM CHANTILLY CREAM

This recipe is an old favourite of mine. It tastes delicious and works perfectly for a fancy dinner party or just as an indulgent weekend dessert. This can be made a day or two in advance and reheated just before serving. If you want to a non-alcoholic version for all the family, substitute grape juice for the red wine.

Peel the pears leaving the stalk intact, then trim the base with a paring knife so they stand upright.

Pour the wine or grape juice into a tight-fitting saucepan and add the sugar, cinnamon, peppercorns and a 7.5-cm/3-in. piece of orange rind, plus a little squeeze of the orange juice (about 1 tablespoon, give or take). Warm the liquid over medium heat, stirring, until the sugar is dissolved, then carefully place the pears into the saucepan – it's okay if they fall over.

Bring to a simmer and poach for 45 minutes, or until the pears are soft with only a little resistance when a knife is inserted. Once cooked, remove the pears from the saucepan (I find a wooden spoon is best to avoid damaging the pears) and leave to cool.

Meanwhile, return the pan to the heat and simmer until the sauce is reduced by half and nice and glossy. You can at this stage pop everything into the fridge and reheat when you want to serve.

Whisk the cream with the icing/confectioners' sugar, vanilla extract and orange blossom extract until you have soft, billowy peaks; don't over-whisk the cream. Taste, adding more orange blossom extract if needed, then cover and chill in the fridge until ready to serve.

To serve, stand a pear proud in a serving bowl. Pour the sauce over the pear to make it glossy, it will pool in the bowl too. If you want to be fancy you can cut a small insertion at the top of the pear and push a mint leaf in, otherwise just scatter a few into each bowl. Serve with a dollop of the orange blossom chantilly cream on the side.

NOTE *If you made this in advance, reheat the pears in the microwave for a minute; just to warm and take the chill off and heat the sauce in a saucepan to warm through.*

**4 conference pears**
**750-ml/3-cup bottle of red wine or red grape juice**
**200 g/1 cup caster/granulated white sugar**
**5-cm/2-in. cinnamon stick**
**12 black peppercorns**
**1 orange**
**a few mint leaves, to garnish**
**Orange Blossom Chantilly Cream, to serve (see below)**

**ORANGE BLOSSOM CHANTILLY CREAM**
**300 ml/1¼ cups double/ heavy cream**
**2 tablespoons icing/ confectioners' sugar**
**a few drops of vanilla extract**
**½ teaspoon orange blossom extract**

**SERVES 4**

# BUTTERNUT SQUASH & ORANGE PIE

An alternative take on the traditional pumpkin pie, my butternut squash and orange pie is great all year round and has a slightly more summery feel with the addition of tangy orange zest. Serve with a dollop of almond-flavoured sweetened cream.

Make the pastry case/pie shell following the recipe on page 31.

After baking the pastry, reduce the oven temperature to 160°C fan/180°C/350°F/gas 4.

Place the squash on a lightly oiled baking sheet and bake for about 40 minutes, or until soft but not coloured. Once done, tip into a large mixing bowl and mash with a potato masher. Leave the oven on.

Use an electric hand whisk to beat the sugar and mashed squash together in a large bowl for a few minutes. Leave to cool slightly then add the eggs and whisk together until fully incorporated. Add the evaporated milk, ginger, vanilla extract, orange zest and a pinch of salt. Whisk until everything has completely combined. Finally fold in the flour, then whisk again until you have a very loose mixture.

Increase the oven temperature to 180°C fan/200°C/400°F/gas 6. Pour the mixture into the pastry case and scatter over the almonds. Bake for 40 minutes, it should be firm but have the slightest of wobbles when shaken. When done, remove from the oven and leave to cool in the tin/pan.

Whisk the cream with the icing/confectioners' sugar and almond extract until you have soft peaks; don't over-whisk the cream. Taste, adding more almond extract if needed, then cover and chill in the fridge until ready to serve.

Slice the pie to serve, with dollops of the almond chantilly cream.

1 x Shortcrust Pastry Tart Case/ Pie Shell (see page 31)*, or use a store-bought one if you are short of time

FILLING
1 butternut squash (you need about 675 g/1½ lb. flesh), peeled and cut into 5-cm/ 2-in. chunks
flavourless oil, for greasing
180 g /1 cup minus 1½ tablespoons dark brown soft sugar
3 eggs
170 g/200 ml evaporated milk
½ teaspoon ground ginger
1 teaspoon vanilla extract
finely grated zest of 1 orange
a pinch of salt
75 g/½ cup plus 1 tablespoon plain/all-purpose flour
2 tablespoons toasted flaked/ slivered almonds

ALMOND CHANTILLY CREAM
300 ml/1¼ cups double/heavy cream
2 tablespoons icing/ confectioners' sugar
a few drops of almond extract

*25-cm/10-in. tart tin/pan*

**SERVES 8**

* You can make the Shortcrust Pastry Case/Pie Shell up to 3 days in advance

# HAZELNUT CHOCOLATE SOUFFLÉS

Baked soufflés are actually easier to make than you might think. My hazelnut and chocolate spread version elevates the more traditional chocolate version and is a huge hit with the kids.

Preheat the oven to 200°C fan/220°C/425°F/gas 7.

Melt about 2 tablespoons of the butter and use it to brush the inside of the ramekins, then dust the insides with a little of the caster/superfine sugar, tipping to ensure they are fully coated. Place on a baking sheet.

Separate the egg yolks from the whites into two large bowls. Whisk the egg whites with the remaining caster/superfine sugar and cream of tartar until you have soft peaks. Set aside.

Melt the remaining butter with a pinch of salt and whisk together with the flour in a saucepan. Cook for 1 minute, then remove from the heat and whisk in the cold milk. Once fully incorporated, return to the heat, whisking continuously, until it bubbles and thickens. Cook for another minute, then remove from the heat.

Place the chocolate in a small microwaveable bowl, add 1 tablespoon milk and microwave for 1 minute to warm it through (you don't need it to be fully melted). Scrape this into the white sauce and whisk to incorporate quickly, followed by the hazelnut chocolate spread and egg yolks. Continue whisking until thick and glossy.

Use a spatula to mix one-third of the meringue into the chocolate sauce; you can be heavy handed with this as this is just preparing it for the remaining meringue. Once incorporated, tip in the rest of the meringue and gently fold it through this time, until the meringue is fully combined, then stop – don't over-work it as you want as much air as possible in the mixture.

Carefully pour this into the prepared ramekins to the very top and run your thumb around the rim to remove any spills. Grate over a little of the toasted hazelnut (but not too much).

Bake in the preheated oven for 13–15 minutes (13 minutes will be gooey in the centre; 15 will be fluffy throughout). As soon as you take them out of the oven, dust icing/confectioners' sugar over the top and grate over more toasted hazelnut if liked. Serve immediately.

45 g/4 tablespoons butter
2 tablespoons caster/superfine sugar
3 eggs
a pinch of cream of tartar
a pinch of salt
25 g/3 tablespoons plain/all-purpose flour
250 ml/1 cup whole/full-fat milk, chilled, plus extra for the chocolate
50 g/2 oz. dark/bittersweet chocolate (minimum 70% cocoa), broken into pieces
200 g/7 oz. hazelnut chocolate spread, such at Nutella
a few whole toasted hazelnuts
1 tablespoon icing/confectioners' sugar

*4 x 200-ml/¾-cup capacity ovenproof ramekins or straight-sided coffee cups*

**MAKES 4**

# GINGERED TREACLE TART

My gingery treacle tart is a combination of spicy fresh ginger and sweet golden syrup. It's utterly delicious and best served with a scoop of creamy vanilla ice cream on the side. This is a take on one of the recipes I cooked during my time taking part in the MasterChef competition.

Make the pastry case/pie shell following the recipe on page 31.

After baking the pastry, reduce the oven temperature to 160°C fan/180°C/350°F/gas 4.

To make the filling, melt the butter in a medium saucepan set over a low heat. Whisk in the golden/corn syrup (keeping the filling slightly warm helps to incorporate the ingredients better). Once combined, remove the pan from the heat and add the breadcrumbs, followed by the beaten eggs and finally, the grated ginger and lemon juice. Mix until combined.

Pour the filling into the pastry case to fill it to the top and bake it in the preheated oven for about 15 minutes, there should still be a slight wobble in the middle (but don't overcook it). Remove from the oven and leave to cool in the tin/pan for about 1 hour.

Sprinkle a small pinch of sea salt flakes over the top just before serving and serve sliced with scoops of vanilla ice cream on the side.

1 x Shortcrust Pastry Tart Case/
Pie Shell (see page 31*), or
use a store-bought one if
you are short on time
a pinch of sea salt flakes,
to garnish
vanilla ice cream, to serve

FILLING
90 g/6½ tablespoons butter
450 g/1⅓ cups golden/light
corn syrup
90 g/1¾ cups fresh white
or brown breadcrumbs
2 eggs
1½ tablespoons finely grated
fresh ginger
½ teaspoon lemon juice

*25-cm/10-in. tart tin/pan*

**SERVES 4**

* *You can make the Shortcrust
Pastry Case/Pie Shell up to
3 days in advance*

# INDEX

# ACKNOWLEDGEMENTS

Where do I even begin? Writing this book is, ironically, like creating the perfect recipe. A group of professionals come together to create the perfect balance of ingredients; all complementing each other; sometimes with contrast, sometimes with effortless like-mindedness. Those ingredients combine and with the helping hand of an incredible publisher you start to cook, taste and tweak, every ingredient contributing to the collective goal of creating something special and unique.

I have many ingredients to thank… The star of my ingredients list is my wife Anna and three children; Eva, Lex and Luca (I'm leaving out the dog – she contributed nothing to this book). Previously my gratitude to my family would be for their support and honest critique, which is still the case; but also for my inspiration. This is their book; the dishes they've eaten over the years and as we naturally do most dinnertimes, touch upon what we're eating, what would make it better – thank you.

I'm also lucky enough to share my work with a bunch of people that are far more talented than me. First is my publisher David Peters who once again had the confidence in me to write our sixth book together at Ryland Peters & Small – thank you David for your trust. Julia Charles, editorial director and friend, who is the best in the business and has been the bedrock of my writing career at RPS; I suspect Julia knows my language, mistakes and unspoken thoughts better than me and always makes a fabulous drinking and dining partner!

The entire design, styling and shoot team is what translates my recipes into the art you see in this book. Headed by talented designer Megan Smith and creative director Leslie Harrington. Food stylist Libby Silbermann, who besides being incredibly talented also coped with my kids running around the shoot with total grace, and Hannah Wilkinson, for the amazing props. And, last but not least, Mowie Kay, our photographer, who has been with me on every book so far and never fails to capture the essence and magic of every dish and still manages to put up with my bad jokes throughout the shoots.

Yvonne Doolan, publicity director, a marketing guru whom I sometimes forget probably has other authors to look after, but is the bridge between my books and you, the reader; without Yvonne; my books would be the best-kept secret.

The saying goes a recipe is only ever as good as its ingredients – and this book had the best in the business. I'm honoured to have worked with you all and remain in awe of the talent I am lucky enough to get to work with.

Theo x